Esther

FOR SUCH A TIME AS THIS

BY CARL ARMERDING

ONE EVENING BOOK

published by

GOOD NEWS PUBLISHERS

Westchester, Illinois 60153

*To my dear sister
Minnie,
faithful and beloved missionary
to
the Indians
of
the great Southwest*

cover design and format
Rose-Mary Fudala

Library of Congress Catalog Card Number 73-92177

Copyright © 1974

published by
GOOD NEWS PUBLISHERS
Westchester, Illinois 60153

All rights reserved
Printed in the United States of America

Contents

page	chapter	
7	**1**	In a Persian Palace
13	**2**	The Quest for a Queen
24	**3**	A Crisis in the Making
32	**4**	Faith and Fate
40	**5**	An Audience with the King
48	**6**	The Rise and Fall of Men
56	**7**	The Second Banquet
64	**8**	A Passion for Souls
77	**9**	The Tables Turned *1-19
86	**9**	Memorial Days *20-32
94	**10**	The Greatness of Mordecai

*corresponds to Bible reference chapter and verse

Introduction

Iran, known as Persia before March, 1935, is the country in which Esther was born and brought up. For many years this country located in the heart of the Middle East had little political importance, but in recent years its affairs have occupied the headlines of our newspapers.

Many people think of the country as the source of Persian rugs. Its chief source of wealth is its oil. According to reliable geologists, "the country fairly floats on oil." But this has also been the source of much of its trouble.

Biblically, Persia is also an important country. In the second chapter of Daniel, often referred to as "the primer of prophecy," we find this country in association with Media taking its place as the second great world empire. Babylon was first. Nebuchadnezzar was told by the prophet Daniel that he was "that head of gold." The capture of the city of Babylon by Cyrus the Persian in the days of Belshazzar marked the end of that empire. It was succeeded by the Medo-Persian Empire, represented in the image or colossus of the second chapter of Daniel as the breast and arms of silver.

In his interpretation of this Daniel speaks of it as an inferior kingdom, Dan. 2:39. It was inferior in that it was not an absolute monarchy like the Babylonian Empire. It is said of Nebuchadnezzar that "whom he would he slew...and whom he would he set up; and whom he would he put down," Dan. 5:19. Such was evidently not the case with the Persian monarch. Before deposing Vashti, for example, we find that he consults with the nobles, Esther 1:13 ff.

In Daniel 7:5 this same kingdom is said to be "like to a bear, and it raised up itself on one side, and it had three ribs in the mouth of it between the teeth of it: and they said thus unto it, Arise, devour much flesh." From this we may gather that this empire was both powerful and rapacious. We find this same kingdom mentioned again in Daniel 8:3 where it is described as "a ram which had two horns: and the two horns were high; but one was higher than the other, and the higher came up last." To this the prophet adds, "I saw the ram pushing westward, and northward, and southward; so that no beasts might stand before him, neither was there any that could deliver out of his hand; but he did according to his will, and became great."

Such was the state of the Persian Empire in the days of Esther. We shall see as we proceed with our study that it was enjoying a period of prosperity. Many thought that this would go on indefinitely, little realizing how soon all might be taken from them. From our "primer of prophecy" we know that it was to be overcome by the Greeks just as the Babylonians had been overthrown by the Medes and the Persians.

Those who make a study of the book of Esther will notice that the name of God is never mentioned in it. Nevertheless we are persuaded that "behind the dim unknown, standeth God within the shadow, keeping watch above His own."

The book of Esther gives us a segment of the history of the Jews which is not supplied elsewhere in the Bible. It is here that we learn about the origin of the *Feast of Purim* which is still celebrated by the Jewish people. There are great moral lessons which may be learned from this book. We may be sure that "whatsoever things were written aforetime were written for our learning, that we through patience and comfort of the scriptures might have hope," Rom. 15:4. With such words of encouragement before us let us proceed with our study, ever counting upon the blessed Spirit of God to guide us into all truth, John 16:13.

CHAPTER ONE *In a Persian Palace*

■ IT WAS the third year of the reign of King Ahasuerus, emperor of vast Media-Persia, with its 127 provinces stretching from India to Ethiopia. This was the year of the great celebration at Shushan Palace, to which the emperor invited all his governors, aides and army officers, bringing them in from every part of Media-Persia for the occasion. The celebration lasted six months, a tremendous display of the wealth and glory of his empire.

When it was all over, the king gave a special party for the palace servants and officials—janitors and cabinet officials alike—for seven days of revelry, held in the courtyard of the palace garden. The decorations were green, white and blue, fastened with purple ribbons tied to silver rings embedded in marble pillars. Gold and silver benches stood on pavements of black, red, white, and yellow marble. Drinks were served in golden goblets of many designs, and there was an abundance of royal wine, for the king was feeling very generous. The only restriction on the drinking was that no one should be compelled to take more than he wanted, but those who wished could have as much as they pleased. For the king had instructed his officers to let everyone decide this matter for himself.

Queen Vashti gave a party for the women of the palace at the same time.[1]

This is the beginning of a drama that was to affect

[1] Esther 1:1-9, *Living Bible*

the fate of the nation of Israel as well as the Persian king, queen and a young girl named Esther.

The king in this account is given the name Ahasuerus. This was probably a royal title rather than a personal name. Most likely he was Xerxes I who reigned in Persia from 485 B.C. until 465 B.C.

Xerxes I succeeded his father Darius and was able to regain Egypt, something which his father had been unable to accomplish. But he failed to conquer Greece, even though he exhausted his empire in the attempt to do so. He was assassinated in 465 B.C., and his son Artaxerxes I succeeded him.

From verse 2 of this chapter we learn that he had his palace in *Shushan* which is indicated as *Susa* on most Bible maps, 150 miles north of the head of the Persian Gulf.

We are not told how many guests there were at the feast but the number would possibly run into hundreds. The list of guests probably changed from time to time, because the feast lasted about six months. Since this great gathering took place previous to Persia's third expedition against Greece in 480-479 B.C. it has been suggested that the real purpose of this gathering was to prepare for that. That seems to be confirmed by the statement that all the king's governors, aides and army officers were there. No doubt they came in relays, because all could not be absent from their official posts at the same time.

According to Herodotus, it was at this feast that he announced his ambition. "As Cyrus, Cambyses, and Darius have enlarged the empire I wish to do the same. I propose to bridge the Hellespont, march through Europe, and fire Athens for burning Sardis and opposing Datis and Artaphernes. By reducing

Attica and Greece, the sky will be the only boundary of Persia." The display of all his riches and glory may have been made at this time both to impress them and to inspire them. Others have tried the same tactics only to find by sad experience that "pride goeth before destruction, and a haughty spirit before a fall," Prov. 16:18.

The second feast lasted only a week and seems to have been made especially for the people living in the palace. The palace was distinct from the city, Esther 9:12, 13. We are not told how many people lived in the palace, only that they were "great and small." It would seem from verse 9 of our chapter that only men were present.

The description of the court of the garden in verse 6 shows what a grand place it must have been with its awnings of various colors. After the manner of the Orient, the guests would recline at the table as they did when our Lord was on earth. The beds, or couches, on which they reclined were of gold and silver. This may mean that the coverings were made of cloth of gold and silver or it may mean that the beds were actually made of the precious metals. But where we might expect to find expensive Persian rugs there was "a pavement of red, and blue, and white, and black, and marble." According to another translation these last two were really alabaster and black marble or mother of pearl.

Evidently the main feature of this feast was the drinking of royal wine of which there was an abundance. The cups from which the guests drank were all of gold, no two alike. But the drinking was without constraint. The reason for this royal commandment was "that they should do according to every man's pleasure." What that "pleasure" meant we may learn from what follows.

In the ninth verse we learn of another feast given by the queen for the women in the royal house which belonged to King Ahasuerus. Possibly Vashti was not the actual name of the queen but an epithet like "sweetheart" or "darling." This would indicate that she was a great favorite of the king.

"On the seventh day," just as the feast for all the people was drawing to a close, "when the heart of the king was merry with wine...he commanded the seven chamberlains that served" in his presence to bring the queen before him "with the crown royal to show the people and the princes her beauty: for she was fair to look upon." Since it was the custom for women to be heavily veiled, she would have to appear unveiled for the king to show her beauty to the men assembled. Evidently this was too much for her. To break with that tradition was too serious a matter to Vashti. Also she probably knew that the king was not the only one whose heart "was merry with wine." To have appeared in such company unveiled would have exposed her to possible insult and disgrace. So she "refused to come at the king's commandment by his chamberlains" or eunuchs.

He who shortly before was merry with wine is "very wroth, and his anger burned in him." However he had enough sense to consult with his "wise men" before taking any action against the queen. We note that these wise men were men which knew the times. They also knew law and judgment. Because of this they enjoyed a place of special nearness to the king, they "saw the king's face," and they also "sat the first in the kingdom." Officially they were "the seven princes of Persia and Media." In our country we would call them members of the

Cabinet. In Great Britain they would be known as the Privy Council.

The fact that these men knew the times may mean that they knew the trends of the day. Possibly Vashti's refusal to obey the command of Ahasuerus was a symptom of a current social movement. Since the wise men had knowledge of the times as well as of the law, they saw that her refusal would have far-reaching effects. Memucan said before the king and the princes, "Vashti the queen hath not done wrong to the king only, but also to all the princes, and to all the people that are in all the provinces of the king Ahasuerus." But there is no evidence that she had broken a law which was in force at that time. Seemingly the men feared that when the news got around that "the king Ahasuerus commanded Vashti the queen to be brought in before him, but she came not," that all the women in the realm would despise their husbands. From verse 18 we learn that they especially feared what might happen in the court itself. If Vashti's refusal should have such effects, some sort of social upheaval may have been developing.

To retain order they proposed that a royal commandment should go out from the king and that it should become a part of the unalterable laws of the Persians and the Medes "that Vashti come no more before king Ahasuerus." This probably was tantamount to life imprisonment. Even though these wise men had the reputation of knowing law and judgment, they did not act according to either on this occasion. Evidently the government of Persia was not the same as the absolute rule of Babylon since this was proposed, not by the king, but by his advisers.

In their advice to the king the wise men not only suggested what should be done to Vashti but they also wanted him to "give her royal estate unto another that is better than she." The purpose of this is clearly indicated in verse 20. "When the king's decree which he shall make shall be published throughout all his empire (for it is great), all the wives shall give to their husbands honor, both to great and small." While the official position of Vashti made her offense more serious than if she had been an ordinary housewife, there was also the grave possibility that her action would touch off a revolt among the women of the day.

"And the saying pleased the king and the princes; and the king did according to the word of Memucan." Apparently it was what he wanted to hear or what *they* wanted to hear because the princes are here again associated with him. And "he sent letters into all the king's provinces, into every province according to the writing thereof, and to every people after their language, of every people." When we consider that there were 127 provinces in the empire, we get some idea of the magnitude of this task. No doubt the decree was translated into a number of different languages. It had to be according to the writing, or script, of each province.

The last part of this royal decree has been interpreted to mean "that every man should speak his own language in his family, and not that of his wife, if that were different. This is the plain meaning of the existing text, which cannot bear either of the senses suggested in the Authorized Version," *Pulpit Commentary*. The American Standard Version merely says "that every man should bear rule in his own house, and should speak according to the language of his people." The new Revised Standard Version is substantially the same.

Vashti was never called to defend herself. Nor does anyone rise up to defend her. We who have lived in a democracy all our lives can hardly conceive of such a thing. But there are many women in our country today who have been dealt with in much the same way. Like Vashti they have suffered in silence even though they might have won a legal battle if they had taken the matter to court. With queenly grace Vashti did not enter this sad affair which had been magnified out of proportion.

It is possible that she learned that "better is a dry morsel, and quietness therewith, than an house full of sacrifices with strife," Prov. 17:1.

CHAPTER TWO *The Quest for a Queen*

■ IN THE STUDY and interpretation of history there is room for diversity of opinion. What seems to be right to one may seem wrong to another. Did Esther do wrong in hiding her identity or was she justified in so doing? Was Mordecai at fault when he charged his cousin not to show" her people nor her kindred?" The best we can do is to carefully study the facts and seek God's help to understand them.

Some believe that there is a lengthy interval between chapters 1 and 2. It would take some time to send letters to all of the king's provinces since means of communication were much slower then than they are now. That would give ample time for the king to reconsider things. We read that "the wrath of king Ahasuerus was appeased." The original word for *appeased* is the same word which is translated *assuaged* in Genesis 8:1. There it refers to the subsiding of the waters of the Flood in the days of Noah. We find it again in Esther 7:10 where it is renderded *pacified*. Now that he was sober and had time to reflect on his actions "he remembered Vashti, and what she had done, and what was decreed against her." Many commentators have detected a note of remorse. He might even have reinstated Vashti, but those who surrounded him would not allow that to happen. The laws of the Medes and Persians could not be changed.

"Then said the king's servants that ministered unto him, Let there be fair young virgins sought for the king." In this way Vashti's royal estate would be given to another better than she. Nothing is said about the social or political qualifications of the prospective queen. Neither is there any reference to the education or training she should have for such a high office. Apparently the only qualifications necessary were physical. She must be a fair young virgin. The proposition differs little from the way in which a movie star might be chosen today. Hollywood is constantly in search of "fresh faces."

The search for a new queen for the Persians extended to the remotest corners of the empire. Elaborate machinery was set up so that no possible candidate would be overlooked. The ministers of Ahasuerus suggested that "the king appoint officers in all the provinces of his kingdom, that they may gather together all the fair young virgins unto Shushan the palace, to the house of the women, unto the custody of Hegai the king's chamberlain, keeper of the women" and that their things for purification be given them. "And let the maiden which pleaseth the king be queen instead of Vashti." Evidently this met with royal approval because we read that "the thing pleased the king; and he did so."

"The house of the women" was what we would call a harem. King Solomon must have had something like this to accommodate his many wives and concubines. Such an institution naturally accompanies polygamy. "Hegai the king's chamberlain" who was in charge probably was the chief eunuch. He "was usually a repulsive old man, on whom the court ladies are very dependent, and whose favour they are always desirous to secure," *Jamieson, Fausset and Brown*. The fact that things were given them for "purification" indicates that the king must have been considered almost divine. "It would have been well if the divinity had been himself less impure," *Pulpit Commentary*. Like many people today they had double standards, one for the king and another for the common people. Many men still demand utmost purity in the girl they expect to marry, but have no thought of offering her as much.

In contrast to all of the above we now have introduced one who is to play an important role in this story. "In Shushan the palace there was a certain Jew, whose name was Mordecai, the son of Jair, the son of Shimei, the son of Kish, a Benjamite." His genealogy was well kept even though he was in exile. He "had been carried away from Jerusalem with the captivity which had been carried away with Jeconiah king of Judah, whom Nebuchadnezzar the king of Babylon had carried away."

According to II Chronicles 36, there were three different deportations of Jews from Jerusalem in the days of Nebuchadnezzar. The first came in the days of Jehoiakim, the second, in the days of his son Jehoiachin and the third, in the days of Zedekiah. No doubt the *Jeconiah* referred to here is the same as *Jehoiachin*, who was taken captive in 597 B.C. If Mordecai was among those carried away at that time, he would now be a very old man. Therefore it has been thought that the first part of verse 6 refers to his ancestor, Kish. Grammatically the pronoun *who* might refer to either one. It is sufficient for us that he was a descendant of Benjamin and thus a member of the tribe from which the first king of Israel was taken.

Evidently Mordecai was a kindly man for "he brought up Hadassah, or Esther, his uncle's daughter: for she had neither father nor mother, and the maid was fair and beautiful; whom Mordecai, when her father and mother were dead, took for his own daughter." This is a lovely touch in a chapter which leaves the impression that women were considered objects which might be shoved around to suit their masters. Mordecai, being a Jew, would know that the law of Moses says, "Ye shall not afflict any widow, or fatherless child," Exod. 22:22. But he did more than the law required. His obedience was not merely negative, it was positive. Some commentators have considered him a type of our Lord Jesus Christ. Here he acted according to the manner of the Lord who "relieveth the fatherless and the widow," Psa. 146:9.

The fact that Esther had two names reminds us of Daniel and his companions. Perhaps she got the name *Esther* in the same way that they got the names by which they were known in the court of Nebuchadnezzar. Her parents had given her the name *Hadassah*, meaning *myrtle*. The name *Esther* was probably derived from *Ishtar*, the chief goddess of the Babylonians and Assyrians. *Ishtar* was the Persian name for the star Venus. If it was Hegai who gave her this name, it may be that she had won his favor and that this name was prophetic of her success in the contest for the queenship.

"So it came to pass, when the king's commandment and his decree was heard, and when many maidens were gathered together unto Shushan the palace, to the custody of Hegai, that Esther was brought also unto the king's house, to the custody of Hegai, keeper of the women." This was no mere beauty contest. These virgins were not invited to compete with each other for a coveted prize. In a modern beauty contest only one can win, but those who loose are free to go their own way. Such was not the case here. No woman would care to go into seclusion for the rest of her life simply because she did not please a capricious man. We can understand why some Jewish commentators thought that Mordecai had tried to keep his cousin out of this, But he had no choice. It was "the king's commandment and his decree."

We are told of *Hegai*, who was in charge of these women, that "the maiden pleased him, and she obtained kindness of him." Here we begin to see the hand of Him who is not even mentioned by name in this book. Although she was favorably received, she had to go through the required procedure for purification. Hegai "speedily gave her her things for purification, with such things as belonged to her," or, "her portions," according to another version.

These portions probably included her food and other necessities. The "seven maidens, which were meet to be given her, out of the king's house," were appointed to attend her in rotation, one for every day of the week.

As a mark of the high esteem in which Hegai held Esther, "he preferred her and her maids unto the best place of the house of the women." (According to the A.S.V., "he removed her," which seems to imply that when she first came into the king's house, she had been assigned to an undesirable place. In this we may see further evidence of the providence of God. We believe that He still works in behalf of His own because there are many favors shown us which we cannot account for except that God has been working in our behalf.)

Meanwhile "Esther had not showed her people nor her kindred: for Mordecai had charged her that she should not show it." It is possible that the primary purpose in hiding her identity was to protect her from violence. She was not "preferred... to the best place of the house of the women" without provoking jealousy. But in due time she will have to reveal who she is. We have had some examples of this in our own day. Before the rise of Hitler in Germany there were many Jews who had become so completely identified with the German people that they were no longer referred to as Jews but as Germans. But we do not question the motives of Mordecai. He was seeking to shield Esther from hatred and violence in a time of anti-Semitism.

Mordecai was not completely at ease even after Esther had been shown favor in the royal harem, for he "walked every day before the court of the women's house, to know how Esther did, and what should become of her." Perhaps he was one of the porters who guarded the entrance to the palace.

What we have here may seem like a waste of time. According to verse 12 of this chapter, it took an entire year to prepare these women for their presentation to the king. Nothing is said about intellectual or spiritual preparation. The phrase "according to the manner of the women" should read, "according to the law for the women," or that which was required by state etiquette. Probably some of the "fair young virgins" had come from homes that were not sanitary. Thus a long season of purification would be required before they might be introduced to his majesty.

These purifications were accomplished first of all "with oil of myrrh" for six months. Myrrh served a double purpose in that it was not only fragrant, but was also credited with having purifying powers. It was an ingredient in the holy anointing oil used in the anointing of the priests in Israel, Exod. 30:22-33. It was among the gifts presented by the Magi when they came from the East to worship our Lord Jesus soon after His birth, Matt. 2:11. It was mingled with the wine which was offered to Him when He was suffering upon the cross, Mark 15:23. Finally it was used at His burial when Nicodemus "brought a mixture of myrrh and aloes, about an hundred pound weight," John 19:39.

Thus myrrh had a variety of uses. But the myrrh that is mentioned here is different from that which is mentioned in Genesis 37:25 and 43:11 where a different word is used in the original. The word used in the book of Esther means "distilling in drops" suggestive of tears. The Persians probably saw no spiritual significance in this. But for the child of

God purification usually is accompanied by tears. But when He who "by Himself purged our sins" comes forth in His royal robes, we are told that all of His garments smell of myrrh and aloes and cassia, Psa. 45:8. Perhaps the Persian custom of purification had its beginnings in what was orginally a divine institution. Such a supposition is not unreasonable because the instructions given to Moses in Exodus 30 antedated this chapter by a thousand years.

In addition to the myrrh there were "sweet odors ...with other things for the purifying of the women." The women were permitted to request whatever else they might think necessary. Possibly some virgins provided themselves with an aphrodisiac to arouse the king's passion. Much was at stake. If a virgin failed to delight him, "she came in unto the king no more." Small reward for a whole year of preparation!

How different the case of one who has prepared himself for the service of the King of Kings! He, too, may be privileged to spend but a short time "on the field." But he will not be cast off on that account. The King will delight in him and he will be "called by name" to enter into the joy of his Lord.

When Esther's turn came "to go in unto the king, she required nothing but what Hegai the king's chamberlain, the keeper of the women appointed." She required no extras to make her more desirable. We are not told if she was anxious about the outcome. "And Esther obtained favor in the sight of all them that looked upon her."

"So Esther was taken unto king Ahasuerus into his house royal in the tenth month, which is the month Tebeth, in the seventh year of his reign." The tenth month here corresponds to the latter part of December and the earlier part of January of our present calendar. This is the only time that "the month Tebeth" is mentioned in Scripture. But the interesting thing about it is that it is also called "the tenth month," which is the tenth month of the Jewish *sacred* year and the fourth month of their *civil* year. Perhaps this is another incidental reference that God is not left without witness. "The tenth month" was dated from the Passover, the great memorial of Israel's redemption from the bondage of Egypt.

"And the king loved Esther above all the women, and she obtained grace and favor in his sight more than all the virgins; so that he set the royal crown upon her head, and made her queen instead of Vashti." This is the only reference to love in this book. It only is here that we find the combination "grace and favor," two words which are frequently used in the Old Testament to describe God's attitude toward His people.

"Then the king made a great feast unto all his princes and his servants, even Esther's feast; and he made a release to the provinces, and gave gifts, according to the state of the king." The fact that this is called "Esther's feast" suggests that this may have been her coronation feast. According to Dr. Jamieson, her crown consisted only of a purple fillet streaked with white, having the appearance of a crown of towers, bound around the forehead. And on the basis of the rendering given in the Septuagint, he says that the feast was really a marriage feast.

According to the *Pulpit Commentary*, the "release" was an exemption from taxation, or from military service, or from both, for a specified period. The word for release is not the same as that used in

Deuteronomy 15 in connection with the year of jubilee. Although much that we find here may simulate the divine pattern, it can never equal the original. This, as well as the giving of gifts, is an illustration of what takes place when we are received by divine grace into God's loving favor. It is said of our Lord that "when he ascended up on high, he led captivity captive, and gave gifts unto men," Eph. 4:8. All of this is "according to the state of the king." When we apply that to the King of kings, we find that no earthly monarch can compare with Him. What happened that day in the Persian palace is like the flicker of a candle in the light of the noonday sun. Our Lord has raised us up together and made us sit together in heavenly places so that in the ages to come He may show the exceeding riches of His grace in His kindness toward us through Christ Jesus, Eph. 2:6, 7.

There is a break at this point of the chapter. A second gathering of virgins probably took place some time after Esther's feast. We are not told the purpose of this gathering. But the fact that "then Mordecai sat in the king's gate" appears as though he had been promoted. Besides the ordinary use of the gates of a city as a place of entry, they were also the place where important business was transacted. We have a good illustration of that in the case of Boaz and the near kinsman when the question respecting Ruth and the inheritance was decided by ten men of the elders of the city who sat there as judges, Ruth 4:1, 2. Lot seemingly occupied a similar position in the city of Sodom, Gen. 19:1.

"Esther had not yet showed her kindred nor her people; as Mordecai had charged her: for Esther did the commandment of Mordecai like as when she was brought up with him." Although she was now queen of the empire, she did not change her attitude toward the one who had raised her when she was left an orphan. Today such obedience and respect have become the exception rather than the rule.

"In those days, while Mordecai sat in the king's gate, two of the king's chamberlains, Bigthan and Teresh, of those which kept the door, were wroth, and sought to lay hand on the king Ahasuerus." This verse seems to confirm that Mordecai was now in a position of trust and honor. That also will explain how he discovered the conspiracy against the life of the king. The two men named in this verse evidently occupied a position of special trust also. If the *Bigthan* mentioned here is the *Bigtha* mentioned in Esther 1:10, then he was one who served in the very presence of the king. Together with Teresh he guarded the door of the king's sleeping apartment, 6:2. Thus they might easily lay hands on the king and kill him.

Some commentators think that they wanted to avenge Vashti and that it was she who instigated this plot. But there is nothing in the sacred record to support that view. They may have confided in a third party who in turn told it to Mordecai. He then "told it unto Esther the queen." She told it to the king "in Mordecai's name."

But judgment was not pronounced on the guilty pair until "inquistion was made of the matter." When "it was found out, they were both hanged on a tree." According to the great historian, Herodotus, this was the punishment usually meted out to rebels and traitors in Persia. The historiographers of that day made a record of the incident in the book of the chronicles of the king. There the matter rested until a later day. Apparently nothing was done for Mordecai at that time. He may have resented that, but his case was in the hands of a higher Judge who saw in secret and one day rewarded him openly.

CHAPTER THREE
A Crisis in the Making

■ IN CHAPTER I a great social upheaval might have occurred if Vashti had not been deposed for her disobedience. Now we see the beginnings of a more serious crisis. Haman is a prototype of modern anti-Semites such as Adolf Hitler and Julius Streicher. But he is not the first. Satan has continually plotted to exterminate the Jew, because the Seed which was to bruise his head was to come through that people. His attempt to frustrate this divine prediction began with the slaughter of Abel by his brother Cain. Pharaoh's attempt to destroy the firstborn of the Israelites was another link in the chain which extends to Calvary and beyond. But Pharaoh did not wish to exterminate the Israelities. He wanted to limit their number so that they could be kept under control. Such was not the case with Haman.

Haman is described as "the son of Hammedatha the Agagite." Most conservative scholars agree the name *Agagite* is a title such as *Pharaoh*. The earliest Biblical reference to Agag is found in the prophecy of Balaam who said of Israel's King that He "shall be higher than Agag, and his kingdom shall be exalted," Num. 24:7. The fact that the Messiah is compared with Agag is significant. The force of this is seen in the prophecies of Balaam who had been hired by Balak, the king of Moab, to curse Israel. Even though Balak had ordered Balaam to flee when he found that instead of cursing Israel he had blessed them three times, Balaam becomes more specific. In his final parable he says, "There shall come a Star out of Jacob, and a Scepter shall smite the corners of Moab, and destroy all the children of Sheth."

When Balaam looked on Amalek he said, "Amalek was the first of the nations; but his latter ends shall be that he perish forever," Num. 24:20. The reason for this is given by Samuel when he said to king Saul, "Thus saith the Lord of hosts, I remember that which Amalek did to Israel, how he laid wait for him in the way when he came up from Egypt. Now go and smite Amalek, and utterly destroy all that they have, and spare them not.... And Saul smote the Amalekites...and he took Agag the king of the Amalekites alive, and utterly destroyed all the people with the edge of the sword. But Saul and the people spared Agag," for which he was sharply rebuked by the prophet who himself "hewed Agag in pieces before the Lord in Gilgal," I Sam. 15:2, 3, 7, 8, 9, 33.

Since the prophecies of Balaam concern "the latter days," Num. 24:14, successors to Agag rose up to frustrate Israel. The Persian Empire in Esther's day included the former kingdom of the Amalekites, "the first of the nations." Haman may have been the heir to the throne of Amalek and for that reason was known as "the Agagite." Even if this title refers primarily to his father, Hammedatha, he would naturally inherit it from him. If Haman was "in the royal line" of the Amalekites, Ahasuerus would advance him to a place above the other princes. From Esther 1:14 we have learned that there were "seven princes of Persia and Media, which saw the king's face, and which sat first in the kingdom." But they were made subordinate to Haman who must have been second only to the king.

"And all the king's servants, that were in the king's gate, bowed, and reverenced Haman: for the king had so commanded concerning him." Since the gates of the city were more than an entrance, the servants were also men of distinction. They may have been former officers in the kingdoms which the Persians had subdued. Since they would consider themselves equal to Haman, the king ordered them to reverence him as their superior.

But there was one among them who refused to obey the royal command. "Mordecai bowed not, nor did him reverence." The other fellows who sat in the gate with him wanted to know why he was transgressing the king's commandment. And "it came to pass, when they spoke daily unto him, and he hearkened not unto them, that they told Haman, to see whether Mordecai's matters would stand: for he had told them that he was a Jew." Perhaps they, too, would like to be excused from bowing to Haman. But they could not use the same reason. Mordecai did not refuse to obey the king's command because he differed with his political views. His reason for disobedience was not a matter of choice for God had made him a Jew. He had lived so long in Persia that he must have become like them. But when the test came, he did not hide his identity even though it might cost him his life.

"And when Haman saw that Mordecai bowed

not, nor did him reverence, then was Haman full of wrath." He was so enraged that "he thought scorn to lay hands on Mordecai alone; for they had showed him the people of Mordecai; wherefore Haman sought to destroy all the Jews that were throughout the whole kingdom of Ahasuerus, even the people of Mordecai." Why the Jews should be referred to as "the people of Mordecai" is not revealed unless Mordecai was now identified as their representative on that council which sat "in the king's gate." No matter what our position may be "none of us liveth to himself, and no man dieth to himself," Rom. 14:7. The Devil hates the Lord's people, not so much because of who they are, but because of what they are. Our Lord Jesus said, "If the world hate you, ye know that it hated me before it hated you. If ye were of the world, the world would love his own: but because ye are not of the world, therefore the world hates you," John 15:18, 19.

All of this happened "in the first month, that is, the month Nisan." Nisan is the seventh month of the civil year and the first of the ecclesiastical or sacred year. It is the same as the month Abib, Exod. 13:4, which the Lord said was to be to them "the beginning of months." It corresponds to our month of April. And it was "in the twelfth year of king Ahasuerus," about five years after the coronation of Esther which took place "in the seventh year of his reign," Esther 2:16.

For one year "they cast Pur, that is, the lot, before Haman." The word *Pur* comes from a primitive root meaning "to crush, to break, and to bring to nought." In order to determine the right day on which to destroy all the Jews, they cast lots. Evidently the lot was called Pur in those days because they used rough stones or pebbles. Perhaps there is some connection between the crushing and the broken pieces used in casting lots. There may be a suggestion of the crushing of the Jewish people.

The Jews themselves used the lot as we know from the ritual of the Day of Atonement, Lev. 16. We read in Proverbs 16:33 that "the lot is cast into the lap; but the whole disposing thereof is of the Lord." Thus we get another incidental touch in this book to show that God is watching over His own.

Having already decided on the day of their destruction, Haman now goes to obtain the royal approval of his bloody scheme. He does not reveal his reasons for desiring the Jews' destruction. He does not even mention Mordecai by name nor bring any charge against him. He states, "There is a certain people scattered abroad and dispersed among the people in all the provinces of thy kingdom." Probably the other subdued nations were kept within their former boundaries. But the Jew is different. Haman uses the very words that James uses when writing to the Jews addressing them as "the twelve tribes scattered abroad." Similarly the Apostle Peter writes to the "the strangers scattered throughout Pontus," etc. God had scattered them like seed that would take root and spring up in unpromising soil. No weapon that was formed against them could prosper.

Haman continued, "their laws are diverse from all people." Thus he unwittingly testified to the distinctiveness of the laws committed to the Jews at Sinai. No matter how far the recipients may be scattered distinction remains. Because the law was divine, it remained intact even though those who received those "lively oracles" had repeatedly broken and even despised them. But there was still some obedience to the law. For example, Mordecai refused to bow down to Haman. If Haman was really an Amalekite, then there would be a natural hatred in the heart of Mordecai for one who represented a bitter enemy of his people.

Haman states, "neither keep they the king's laws: therefore it is not for the king's profit to suffer them." Had he carefully considered the Jews' past history as a nation, he would never have said this! Those nations which have not tolerated them have been the losers. But the nations which have favored them have been blessed.

Haman does not allow the king to decide their fate even though he is polite enough to say, "If it please the king." He desires that it "be written that they may be destroyed." And he stands ready to "pay ten thousand talents of silver into the hands of those that have charge of the business, to bring it into the king's treasuries." Since the royal treasuries were exhausted because of the campaign against the Greeks, this would be welcome news. A talent of silver was worth about $2,000. Therefore ten thousand talents would be worth about twenty million dollars! We are not told where Haman was to get this vast sum, but we may get a hint later.

By entrusting his ring to Haman, the king was giving Haman's bloody plan royal sanction. But the Scripture carefully notes that the king "gave it unto Haman the son of Hammedatha the Agagite, the Jews' enemy." There is significance in this repeated description of Haman.

In addition to the royal ring we read that the

silver was given to him and the people also, to do with them as he liked. "The silver" cannot refer to the silver which Haman had offered to pay the king, since it had not yet been paid. It probably refers to the silver of the people whom he now had the authority to exterminate. The confiscation of their goods would naturally follow their liquidation. In giving Haman their silver the king was being generous with that which was not his. Bankrupt though he was, he had to keep up the appearance of affluence.

No plan for the evangelization of the world was ever carried out with more precision than Haman's scheme. "Then were the king's scribes called on the thirteenth day of the first month, and there was written according to all that Haman had commanded unto the king's lieutenants, and to the governors that were over every province, and to the rulers of every people of every province according to the writing thereof, and to every province according to the writing thereof, and to every people after their language." The thirteenth day of the first month would be the day before the Passover lamb had to be killed. By using the royal scribes to write the proclamation, Haman would be spared the personal expense of such a gigantic undertaking.

But there may have been many scribes waiting for something to do. The lieutenants, governors and rulers mentioned in this verse probably refer to the three grades of officers. The highest of these would be the lieutenants, or satraps, "the official title of the viceroy, who, in behalf of the Persian monarch, exercised the civil and military authority in several small provinces combined in one government," *Dictionary of the Bible*, by Davis. The governors would be subordinate to these, whereas the rulers were "native authorities—the head men of the conquered peoples, to whom the Persian system allowed a considerable share of power," *Pulpit Commentary*. Not one province was overlooked. The decree was translated into the language of each province so that everyone would know what was to be expected. If only we communicated the Gospel in such a way! All of this was done in the name of King Ahasuerus and sealed with his ring, the seal in this case being the equivalent of his personal signature.

From verse 13 we learn the contents of this fateful document. "The letters were sent by posts into all the king's provinces, to destroy, to kill, and to cause to perish, all Jews, both young and old, little children and women, in one day, even upon the thirteenth day of the twelfth month, which is the month Adar, and to take the spoil of them for a prey." As we read these words, we are reminded of a modern legal document. The objectives are stated so that there may be no way of escape for any who dare to contest its meaning. The "posts" who carried these letters to the different provinces were couriers who traveled on horseback from one station to another, fresh riders and fresh horses being provided to cover the longer distances. If they had had all the means of communication which we now have, they would have used them. Should we do less to get out the Gospel to every creature?

In verse 14 we come to the publishing of the commandment to all the people. This is the third step in connection with this document. First it was written. Then it was delivered. And finally it was published. The couriers, "hastened by the king's commandment," lost no time in delivering it. The fact that "the decree was given in Shushan the palace" shows that it came from headquarters. The king and Haman are so confident that the orders will be faithfully carried out that they can sit down with all leisure to drink.

"But the city Shushan was perplexed." "The city" probably was distinct from "the palace." The common people were evidently filled with apprehension. Although only Jews were involved this time, it might be their turn next. History has repeatedly shown that the fate of Gentiles has been bound up with the fate of the Jews. Even if every Jew in the country were destroyed, the murderer would soon be looking for fresh victims. He is well named Apollyon, the Destroyer.

CHAPTER FOUR
Faith and Fate

■ FEW PEOPLE WILL survey the whole state of affairs when they get into trouble. Some completely lose their head while others try to "muddle through." As one considers Mordecai's situation, one wonders what other course he might have pursued had he anticipated all that resulted from his refusal to bow down to Haman. In the first verse of this chapter he seemed quite surprised, for when he "perceived all that was done, Mordecai rent his clothes, and put on sackcloth with ashes."

According to Revelation 6:12, sackcloth was black. It was usually made of goats' hair and garments made of it "probably ressembled a sack, with openings made for the neck and arms, and slit down the front...and usually worn over other raiment, but sometimes next to the skin," *Dictionary of the Bible*. According to one authority, such garments were not even removed at night. In those days sackcloth was the customary attire of mourners. But it was also worn at times by prophets and frequently captives were dressed in sackcloth. Thus is was symbolic of sorrow, humility and humiliation.

In the story of Joseph, when his brother Reuben discovered that he was no longer in the pit into which his brothers had cast him, he "rent his clothes" as a sign of grief. When Jacob received Joseph's coat, which had been dipped in blood to make it appear that some wild beast had devoured him, he also "rent his clothes, and put sackcloth upon his loins, and mourned for his son many days," Gen. 37:29-34. Likewise the prophet Daniel set his face unto the Lord his God in prayer and supplication "fasting, and sackcloth, and ashes," Dan. 9:3.

Mordecai possibly knew what Daniel had done and finding himself in similar circumstances did likewise. Evidently he still believed that he had done right in refusing to bow down to Haman. That seems to confirm the view that his refusal was based on religious grounds even though no reference is made to that. In any case he made no secret of his grief, for he "went out into the midst of the city, and cried with a loud and bitter cry." It has been suggested that Esther and Mordecai, as well as all the other Jews in Persia at that time, could have avoided this trouble if they had returned to their own land when King Cyrus gave them permission to leave. But who can say that Haman would not have pursued them there as well?

In the days of Daniel the Chaldeans accused the Jews because they would not fall down and worship the golden image which King Nebuchadnezzar had set up. As a result Shadrach, Meshach and Abednego were cast into a fiery furnace which had been heated seven times more than usual. Thus anti-Semitism was not a new thing. Indeed Mordecai may have remembered all of this when he refused to bow down to Haman. Even though he and his compatriots did not return to their own land when they had the opportunity, the Lord made even that to work out for their good and His glory.

Mordecai had no desire to hide his grief, for he "came even before the king's gate," which none could enter who were clothed with sackcloth. Thank God, such is not the case with the King of Kings! The child of God is bidden to come boldly to His throne of grace in order that he may obtain mercy and find grace to help in time of need, Heb. 4:16. Although Mordecai could not come to the throne of King Ahasurerus, he went as far as he could. In so doing he was actually representing his people. "In every province wherever the king's decree came there was great mourning among the Jews, and fasting, and weeping and wailing: and many lay in sackcloth and ashes."

The news finally reached Queen Esther. But it was not Mordecai who informed her. Her own "maids and her chamberlains" told her and she was "exceedingly grieved." The chamberlains were eunuchs appointed by the king to wait on her. Seemingly neither the maids nor the chamberlains knew why Mordecai was in trouble. Neither did the queen inquire at first. But she did send "raiment to clothe

Mordecai, and to take away his sackcloth from him: but he received it not." In light of what our Lord Jesus said about fasting in His Sermon on the Mount, it may be thought that Mordecai should have received the clothing from the queen. But our Lord was not speaking of true mourners when He said, "When ye fast, be not, as the hypocrites, of a sad countenance: for they disfigure their faces, that they may appear unto men to fast." Mordecai was no hypocrite.

Then the queen sent one of the king's chamberlains to "know what it was, and why it was" that Mordecai acted this way. "So Hatach went forth to Mordecai unto the street of the city, which was before the king's gate." Apparently the king's decree had not been published within the palace. If it had, then surely Hatach and the queen would have known the cause of Mordecai's grief. Probably even Haman did not realize that the decree would affect anyone in the palace. The Apostle Paul, speaking of the wisdom of God, said that none of the princes of this world knew it, for had they known it, they would not have crucified the Lord of glory, I Cor. 2:8. No doubt Satan knows a great deal, but he is not omniscient. In spite of his many defeats he repeatedly tries to destroy that which is indestructible. Long before the days of Mordecai the Lord said of Israel, "No weapon that is formed against thee shall prosper," Isa. 54:17.

In the public square which was before the king's gate Mordecai told Hatach "all that had happened unto him and of the sum of the money that Haman had promised to pay to the king's treasuries for the Jews, to destroy them." Since Haman in his conference with the king had merely stated that there was "a certain people" which it was "not for the king's profit to suffer" or permit to exist, this information would reveal the identity of that "certain people." That a sum of money was involved might also answer any question concerning the king's readiness to grant Haman's request. "The king's profit" and not Haman's hatred of Mordecai was made the excuse for this murderous plot. To confirm all of this Mordecai gave Hatach "the copy of the writing of the decree that was given at Shushan to destroy them."

Mordecai not only asked Hatach to deliver this document to Queen Esther, but "to declare it unto her." In explaining the matter Hatach would make it clear to her that she was involved, as well as Mordecai and the rest of the Jews. What a surprise that would be to her. The laws of the Medes and the Persians were immutable. And the royal seal that made this decree effective was none other than that of Ahasuerus.

Mordecai's charge must have sounded bold indeed. Esther was charged to go before the king "to make supplication unto him, and to make request before him for her people." Mordecai did not suggest an alternative. Neither did he make it optional. "And Hatach came and told Esther the words of Mordecai." Little did she dream what she asked for when she sent Hatach "to know what it was, and why it was!" However it would afford her an unusual opportunity to use her royal office for the salvation of thousands of her people.

As Christians we have been brought to a royal estate through the grace of our Lord Jesus Christ. Some of our fellow Christians who "have obtained like precious faith with us," II Peter 1:1, are being persecuted for His name's sake. We are taught in the Word of God that if one member of the Body of Christ suffers, all the members suffer with it, I Cor. 12:26. Therefore it is our duty to use our royal privileges in making intercession for them. The ears of our Lord are always open to the cries of His own and He heareth and delivereth them, Psa. 34:15, 17. That was no mere theory with the Psalmist, for when he was "in a great strait" he said, "Let me fall now into the hand of the Lord; for very great are his mercies: but let me not fall into the hands of man," I Chron. 21:13.

The Jews certainly were in the hands of men at that time. But He who delivered them in order to chasten them did not cease to care for them. He allowed things to happen so that even the most sanguine might give up in despair. But it is just at that point that He intervenes for their deliverance.

It seems that Esther saw no farther than the king. Note how often she mentions him in her message to Mordecai. She commands Hatach to say: "All the king's servants, and the people of the king's provinces, do know, that whosoever, whether man or woman, shall come unto the king into the inner court, who is not called, there is one law of his to put him to death, except such to whom the king shall hold out the golden scepter, that he may live: but I have not been called to come in unto the king these thirty days." But "the king's heart is in the hand of the Lord, as the rivers of water: he turneth it whithersoever he will," Prov. 21:1. If only Esther had recognized that fact. Then instead of having her eyes on a mere man she would have endured as seeing Him who is invisible, Heb. 11:27.

When her message came to Mordecai, he quickly replied, "Think not with thyself that thou shalt escape in the king's house, more than all the Jews." She must have been shocked when she heard that she would be treated no better than the rest of the Jews. Evidently the edict made no exceptions. But she was not to consider that a calamity, but an opportunity to use her royal position in a wonderful way to save her people.

From the words of Mordecai we gather that he believed that deliverance would come, if not through Esther, then through someone else. He said to her, "If thou altogether holdest thy peace at this time, then shall there enlargement and deliverance arise to the Jews from another place." Surely he must have known that well-known verse, "My help cometh from the Lord, which made heaven and earth," Psa. 121:2.

Previous to this Mordecai had charged Esther not to make known her people or her kindred. This is referred to twice in one chapter, Esther 2:10, 20. But the circumstances have changed since then. The time had come to speak out boldly and conceal nothing. Mordecai was sure that relief would come, but he warned Esther that neither she nor her father's house would share in it if she did not act now. "Who knoweth whether thou art come to the kingdom for such a time as this?" Mordecai told her.

No verse in all the book of Esther is referred to more often than this one. Such a suggestion would be far more powerful than all the threats that he might make. She probably never had considered herself a woman of destiny. But she was. Adapting a text from another part of Scripture we might say, "There were many maidens in Israel in those days and yet to none of them did this opportunity come, save to Esther."

Whether it was this challenge or fear for her own life that moved Esther we do not know. But she did as Mordecai charged her. So she "bade them return Mordecai this answer, Go, gather together all the Jews that are present in Shushan, and fast ye for me, and neither eat nor drink three days, night or day; I also and my maidens will fast likewise; and so will I go in unto the king, which is not according to the law: and if I perish, I perish."

Evidently Mordecai approved this plan, he did what Esther had commanded him. The number of Jews in Shushan must have run into the hundreds, because we learn from chapter 9 that they slew about eight hundred of their enemies in the palace and the city. It would take quite a force to accomplish such a feat. However much they may have been separated from each other before, the fact that they faced a common foe united them as nothing else could.

Queen Esther had resigned herself to fate. Her final word to Mordecai was, "If I perish, I perish." For her everything depended on whether the king would hold out the golden scepter. "No other writer tells us of this custom, but it is in perfect harmony with oriental habits and modes of thought. Some have objected that the king would not always have a golden scepter by him; but the Persepolitan sculptures uniformly represent him with a long staff in his hand, which is probably the scepter," *Pulpit Commentary*. Legally Esther had no right to enter the royal presence unless called. But she had "not been called to come in unto the king these thirty days." That was why she said, "If I perish, I perish."

At this point the sacred historian notes that "Mordecai went his way, and did according to all that Esther had commanded him." He does not seem anxious about the outcome. Although nothing is mentioned about his faith in God, he behaved like a believer in contrast to Esther who apparently was not too hopeful. It truly was a dark hour for all the Jews. But the dawn of a better day was not far off.

CHAPTER FIVE
An Audience with the King

■ WE ARE SO ACCUSTOMED to arranging interviews by mail or telephone that all of the details of this chapter may seem tedious. But we must remember that things were done differently in an Oriental court. Even today some follow much the same procedure in their regular life. Americans traveling in countries to the south of our own find ways of doing things that are quite different from our hasty habits.

I remember one occasion in Palestine when I wanted to make certain purchases before leaving for England. Not knowing the Arabic language, I accepted the kind services of a Christian woman in Jerusalem who knew the language and customs of the people. Together we went to the business section of the old city of Jerusalem. There we found exactly what was wanted. I thought it would only take a few minutes to complete the purchase and be on our way. But I soon discovered that it would not have been the proper thing to do. So we sat down and leisurely talked about our business. When we inquired about the price, it seemed quite exorbitant.

After more talk, the price was reduced to a point where I was ready to close the deal. But my friend urged more patience. After more bargaining, all concerned seemed satisfied. When we prepared to leave, we were showered with words of thanks by the proprietor who enjoyed the occasion more than we had.

That morning, as we left, we recalled the story of Abraham's purchase of the cave of Machpelah as recorded in Genesis 23. His wife Sarah had died and he wanted to buy a burial place. Under such circumstances it might have seemed proper to dispense with formality. But even in a time of sorrow and bereavement, things must be done according to the custom of the country. Some things must be done in a quiet and deliberate way if we are to derive the greatest possible blessing from them. If Esther had rushed through this whole affair, she probably would never have achieved her purpose.

Esther's preparation for her audience with the king will also teach us a lesson. For three days she fasted with her maidens. Then she put on her royal apparel. She knew that no one could enter the king's presence dressed in sackcloth.

In keeping with his station, as well as her own, she dressed like a queen. Even though she came as a suppliant, she never forgot that the king himself had promoted her to a place of honor.

Should we do less when we come to have an audience with the King of kings? Has He not lifted us as beggars from the dunghill to set us among princes? I Sam. 2:8. And has He not provided us with the royal garments of salvation which are suited to His holy presencet? Matt. 2:12. Therefore we may sing with one of old, "I will greatly rejoice in the Lord, my soul shall be joyful in my God; for he hath clothed me with the garments of salvation, he hath covered me with the robe of righteousness, as a bridgegroom decketh himself with ornaments, and as a bride adorneth herself with her jewels," Isa. 61:10.

Notice the gradual way in which Esther approached the royal presence. She first took her stand "in the inner court of the king's house, over against the king's house." Her visit was well timed. "The king sat upon his royal throne, over against the gate of the house." If she had planned months in advance, it could not have been more favorably arranged. Is not that another evidence of the providence of God? Even though Ahasuerus was a heathen king, he may serve as an illustration of the One who is always in readiness to receive us when we draw near to His throne.

"And it was so, when the king saw Esther the queen standing in the court, that she obtained favor in his sight: and the king held out to Esther the golden scepter that was in his hand." It is written, "The king's wrath is as the roaring of a lion; but his favor is as the dew upon the grass," Prov. 19:12. Esther feared the former, but, by God's grace, she experienced the latter. Those three days of fasting and waiting were not in vain.

It may seem strange that Esther should chose this method of gaining an audience with the king since she was his wife. However we must not judge her conduct by modern standards, but according to the customs of those days. History confirms that she followed the only course that was open to her. Mordecai had not specified how she was to approach the king. She had to plan that herself. Imagine her relief as she drew near and touched the top of the extended scepter, the token of royal favor.

"Then said the king unto her, What wilt thou, queen Esther? and what is thy request? It shall be even given thee to the half of the kingdom." He sensed immediately that this was more than a normal call. Nobody would understand more than he that Esther had risked her life in order to secure this brief interview. By extending his scepter and addressing her as queen, he made her doubly sure that he was ready to listen to her request.

Note that he does not say, "What have you to tell me?" He was not only in a listening mood, he was in a giving mood. Queen Esther might have asked for the head of Haman. But the time had not yet come for that. So she simply replies, "If it seem good unto the king, let the king and Haman come this day unto the banquet that I have prepared for him." Note that she makes this a matter of the king's pleasure. She already had prepared this banquet, not for Haman, but for the king.

Esther must have believed that somehow her request would be granted. Oh, that we had similar faith when we come to the Lord with our petitions! Only three days before this she had said, "If I perish, I perish." Evidently those days of fasting were days of reflection. It takes more than abstinence from food to produce so profound a change as this. Although the Lord is not mentioned by name here, His Holy Spirit was quietly working in the heart and mind of Esther.

In contrast to the quiet and deliberate manner of Queen Esther, the king says, "cause Haman to make haste, that he may do as Esther hath said. So the king and Haman came to the banquet that Esther had prepared." A man in his position could easily have found some good reason for not attending a banquet. No doubt matters of state were awaiting his attention. Once again we see the hand of God clearing the way for His child. All the affairs of the Persian Empire are only "a drop of a bucket, and are counted as the small dust of the balance," Isa. 40:15, by "the everlasting God, the Lord, the Creator of the ends of the earth." Yet He upon whom the universe depends is never too busy to receive us and to hear us as we give to Him our petitions.

At the banquet again it was the king who took the initiative when he asked Esther, "What is thy petition?" And again he repeated the promise that her request would be granted even to the half of his kingdom. But this time all of this took place in the hearing of Haman. Knowing something of the urgency of the matter in hand, we cannot but marvel at the self-restraint of Esther. Her only request is that the king and Haman should come to the banquet that she was going to prepare for them on the next day. At that time she would finally make known her real request.

Little did any present at that banquet realize how this postponement would work to Esther's advantage. What if she had been in a hurry? When she postponed her request, she did better than she knew. Of course it may be argued that it was nothing but fear that held her back. The request she was to make involved the king's favorite who was the guest of honor at that banquet. Hatch had brought her the information from Mordecai that "Haman had promised to pay to the king's treasuries for the Jews, to destroy them." It is not difficult to imagine how we would feel if we were confronted by one who had plotted to destroy our loved ones. When she thought of this high position, it might well make her hesitate. But if she had any fears, she did not manifest them. Wonderful things were to happen within the next few hours which would abundantly justify Esther's course. But she knew nothing of these at the moment.

Evidently Haman never suspected what was in store for him. He "went forth that day joyful and with a glad heart." But his joy was soon clouded. When he "saw Mordecai in the king's gate, that he stood not up, nor moved for him, he was full of indignation against Mordecai." It is amazing that a man of Mordecai's comparatively humble standing should cause so much disturbance. Yet his attitude toward Haman is the cause of trouble which soon affects thousands of others. For some reason Haman may have considered him as one who occupied a key position. In that respect he may be typical of the Jewish people. Their importance in the world today is disproportionate to their total number as compared with the population of the world.

If the wise men who came from the East when Christ was born had asked, "Where is He that is born king of the Egyptians?" or, "Where is He that is born king of the Greeks?" their question would probably have stirred up little interest. But when they asked, "Where is he that is born king of the Jews?" Herod was troubled and all Jerusalem with him. The flight into Egypt was ordered, because Herod sought the young Child to destroy Him, Matt. 2:13. Haman's hatred of Mordecai and his plot to destroy him and his people are just episodes in Satan's program of destruction. That program will find its great climax in the Tribulation when the dragon, that is Satan, makes war with the remnant of Israel with a view to their total annihilation, Rev. 12:9-17. Of course Haman was not aware of this. He was only an instrument for "that old serpent, the devil," who knew that out of "the people of Mordecai" would come One who would seal his doom.

As for Haman, we read that he "refrained himself." Apparently as he passed through the gate he never revealed that Mordecai did not rise up to honor him. Since he was next to the king it would be improper for him to explode in public. Also it would have hindered his plan to destroy all the Jews if he had manifested his anger there. But to provide himself with an escape from his anger, when he came home "he sent and called for his friends, and Zeresh his wife, and Haman told them of the glory of his riches, and the multitude of his children, and all the things wherein the king had promoted him, and how he had advanced him above the princes and servants of the king."

To cap it all, he mentions that Esther the queen had not permitted anyone to attend the banquet that she had prepared that day except himself. And he hastens to add, "Tomorrow am I invited unto her also with the king." But there was one thing that spoiled it all. "All this availeth me nothing, so long as I see Mordecai the Jew sitting at the king's gate." It was more than his pride could take.

"Then said Zeresh his wife and all his friends unto him, Let a gallows be made of fifty cubits high, and tomorrow speak thou unto the king that Mordecai may be hanged thereon: then go thou in merrily with the king unto the banquet." This suggestion so unanimously agreed upon shows how cheap human life can be. There was no thought of disposing of Mordecai quietly. Since the Persians did not execute criminals by hanging them, probably the word for *gallows* should be rendered a *pale* or a *cross*. It was by impalement that the Persians punished rebels and traitors in those days, Esther 2:23.

The fact that this "gallows" was to be fifty cubits high, or about 75 feet, has led some commentators to believe that there may be some error in the text. Since letters were used in place of numbrs, that would not be impossible. It might also mean that the pale, or cross, was to be placed high up in a prominent place so that all might see it. That was the case when our blessed Lord was crucified. Their decision to make a public example of Mordecai probably was calculated to strike terror in the hearts of the Jews. Haman could then go in merrily with the king to the banquet. With Mordecai out of the way the main obstacle to his happiness would be eliminated. There were those who thought that by crucifying the Lord Jesus they could get rid of Him also. But it did not work out that way.

So "the thing pleased Haman; and he caused the gallows to be made." Little did he dream that he was preparing for his own execution. He is not the only one who will one day discover that his final doom is of his own execution. Despising the riches of God's goodness and forbearance and longsuffering, men today treasure up to themselves "wrath against the day of wrath and revelation of the righteous judgment of God; who will render to every man according to his deeds," Rom. 2:4-6.

CHAPTER SIX The Rise and Fall of Men

■ HISTORY CONSISTS of the rise and fall of nations and individuals. The Bible gives many illustrations of this fact. But it also gives us the moral reason: "God is the judge: he putteth down one, and setteth up another, Psa. 75:7. King Nebuchadnezzar had to learn that by bitter experience. Even though he was the "head of gold," Dan. 2:38, the first and greatest of a long line of emperors, he had to learn that it was the God of Heaven who had given him "a kingdom, power, and strength, and glory." After the humbling experience having to live in the open fields like a beast for seven years, he lifted up his eyes to Heaven and his understanding returned unto him. Then he blessed the Most High and praised and honored Him who lives forever, who not only rules among men on the earth, but who also "doeth according to his will in the army of heaven ...and none can stay his hand, or say unto him. What doest thou?" Dan. 4:34, 35.

This chapter gives us another striking illustration of this. In chapter 3 we saw the promotion of Haman. Instead of using that advancement for the blessing of others, he became proud and haughty. How truly the Bible states, "Pride goeth before destruction, and an haughty spirit before a fall," Prov. 16:18! And "when pride cometh, then cometh shame," Prov. 11:2. This chapter also gives us a good illustration of the text which says, "Them that honor me I will honor," I Sam. 2:30.

We may have wondered why Esther was so slow in presenting her request to the king even when she had the opportunity. Although that was the proper manner of the Orient, there was a deeper reason. The hand of the Lord was in that apparent delay. It was part of His divine plan to humble the arrogant Haman. Of course He could have smitten Haman with a fatal illness or He might have brought upon him some other adversity. But if He had, then some might have explained his downfall as nothing more than an unhappy circumstance which might have happened to anyone.

The action begins in the bedchamber of the king. "On that night could not the king sleep." Nothing is said about the cause of his insomnia. It is written, "The sleep of a laboring man is sweet, whether he eat little or much: but the abundance of the rich will not suffer him to sleep," Eccles. 5:12. If this Ahasuerus was the wealthy Xerxes of secular history, it is quite possible that the abundance of his riches did not permit him to sleep. How different was the case of the Psalmist who said, "I will not give sleep to mine eyes, or slumber to mine eyelids, until I find out a place for the Lord, an habitation for the mighty God of Jacob," Psa. 132:4, 5. It was not such glorious purpose as this that kept Ahasuerus awake that night. He who neither slumbers nor sleeps, Psa. 121:3, 4, the ever watchful Keeper of Israel, was present in the royal bedchamber that night. The king's heart was in His hand to turn it wherever He willed, Prov. 21:1. With Nebuchadnezzar He used dreams "wherewith his spirit was troubled, and his sleep brake from him," Dan. 2:1.

In the case of Darius whose "sleep went from him," Dan. 6:18, we again see the hand of that same One who ever watches over His own.

Sedatives presumably were known in those days. But Ahasuerus did not order one. He called in no physician nor a minstrel to play for him. "He commanded to bring the book of records of the chronicles; and they were read before the king." "It has been a custom with Eastern kings, in all ages, frequently to cause the annals of the kingdom to be read to them. It is resorted to, not merely to while away the tedium of an hour, but a source of instruction to the monarch, by reviewing the important incidents of his own life, as well as those of his ancestors," *Jamieson, Fausset and Brown*. "And it was found written, that Mordecai had told of Bigthana and Teresh, two of the king's chamberlains, the keepers of the door, who sought to lay hand on the king Ahasuerus." Ahasuerus knew about this when it happened, but he did nothing to reward Mordecai then. Ahasuerus owed his life to Mordecai. In that sense he was his savior even though he was not recognized as such.

There are many who have been saved from something worse than Ahasuerus' fate, but they know so little about their Savior. Apparently they take Him for granted. They may even sing about what He has done for them. But they forget that salvation is more than a great work which has been accomplished for us. When the aged Simeon gazed into the face of the Babe Jesus he said to God, "Mine eyes have seen thy salvation," Luke 2:30. To him salvation was more than something, it was Someone.

The rediscovery of Mordecai by Ahasuerus should teach all believers that importance of becoming better acquainted with the One who has saved us. He has not only saved us from the eternal consequences of our sins, but He continually saves us as we walk through a world that is filled with perils and dangers, seen and unseen. Oh, that there was more searching of "the book of the records" so that we might become increasingly aware of this and, like Ahasuerus, do something about it! Just as Ahasuerus inquired, "What honor and dignity hath been done to Mordecai for this?" so also may we inquire concerning our Lord Jesus, "What honor and dignity have I brought to Him who has done so much for me?" God forbid that people might say we have done nothing for Him! Just as the king was preparing to honor Mordecai, Haman arrived. Such a coincidence is striking, but not unique. Haman probably was unaware of what was happening. But the one of whom he is a type is very wise. Satan always seeks to prevent the honoring of any of God's saints. Likewise he will do all in his power to keep us from bringing honor to the name of the Lord Jesus. Thus Haman's arrival at the court of Ahasuerus is significant. Probably he had passed a sleepless night also. His workmen may have been busy most of the night preparing the gallows on which he hoped to hang Mordecai the next day. All he needed now was the royal permission to carry out his nefarious plan.

The king asks, "Who is in the court?" "And the king's servants said unto him, Behold, Haman standeth in the court. And the king said, Let him come in." Apparently Haman did not have to go through the formality of waiting for the extended scepter as did Queen Esther. On the other hand, the king did not give him a chance to present his request. Without even waiting to say, "Good morning," he says to

Haman, "What shall be done unto the man whom the king delighteth to honor?"

The king did not explain to Haman why he was asking him this question. He gave no hint of "the man" whom he wished to honor. Haman was so self-occupied that he did not inquire who it might be. With utter selfishness he "thought in his heart, To whom would the king delight to do honor more than to myself?" His pride robbed him of ordinary prudence as it so often does. Once again we see the hand of the Lord who "taketh the wise in their own craftiness," Job 5:13 and I Cor. 3:19. Haman clearly knew nothing of that spirit manifested by the Apostle Paul who esteemed others better than himself, Phil. 2:3.

In his ready reply to the king he shows no reserve. He covets the honor of royalty itself. "For the man whom the king delighteth to honor" he would have them bring forth not only royal apparel, but "the royal apparel which the king useth to wear." Neither did he want a horse like the king's horse but the very "horse that the king rideth upon." Then to cap it all, he suggests "the crown royal which is set upon his head." These things were to "be delivered to the hand of one of the king's most noble princes." No ordinary chamberlain would be good enough to "array the man whom the king deligheth to honor."

To complete the picture they were to bring "the man" on horseback through the street of the city with a herald proclaiming before him, "Thus shall it be done to the man whom the king delighteth to honor." Blinded by pride, Haman could see no one but himself in that place of honor. But the king must have known that Haman was speaking for himself. There is humor in this ironical situation.

In his reply to Haman the king said nothing about the crown royal. If he had granted that, people might have assumed that Ahasuerus had transferred his royal authority and dignity to another. Possibly Haman would have assumed that. One as selfish as he would stop at nothing short of the throne itself.

"Then the king said to Haman, Make haste, and take the apparel and the horse, as thou hast said, and do even so to Mordecai the Jew, that sitteth at the king's gate: let nothing fail of all that thou hast spoken." We wonder whether Haman displayed any emotion when he heard that statement. Knowing the real purpose for which he had come to the palace, it is amazing how he could control himself so well. Whatever his feelings were, he did not debate with the king. He did not even beg to be excused.

"Then took Haman the apparel and the horse, and arrayed Mordecai, and brought him on horseback through the street of the city, and proclaimed before him, Thus shall it be done unto the man whom the king delighteth to honor." According to the commandment of the king, he proclaimed all that he had spoken. He dared not disobey even though to obey meant personal dishonor.

But what about Mordecai? He received all of this in silence. He must have been as surprised as Haman. But he had said to Esther that deliverance would arise. That which Haman was ordered to do began the fulfillment of his prediction. In all of this we see a foreshadowing of Satan himself when he is made to bow the knee before Our Lord Jesus. And not only that, the Lord has promised His own that He will make the synagogue of Satan come and worship before their feet to prove that He has loved His own, Rev. 3:9.

The patience and faithfulness of Mordecai was abundantly rewarded. What if he had yielded to Haman? Think of what he would have lost! We are not thinking only of the temporal honor bestowed upon Mordecai. In a much higher sense the Lord was honoring one who had honored Him. The fact that he received all of this in silence is significant. He had nothing to boast of in himself. His behavior would seem to indicate that he recognized that. He did not allow these things to puff him up with pride. Haman's promotion "went to his head." Such was not the case with Mordecai. With grace and modesty he carried his honors well. When the procession was over "Mordecai came again to the king's gate." Apparently he resumed his former position as if he had been used merely as an illustration of one "whom the king delighteth to honor."

"But Haman hasted to his house mourning, and having his head covered." His head covering was probably a veil which was a mark of mourning in those days. It would be a sign to the family of Haman that something dreadful had happened to the head of that household. "And Haman told Zeresh his wife and all his friends everything that had befallen him." It was a great contrast to what he had hoped to tell them on his return from the palace. When he left them not many hours before, he was told by his wife to go merrily with the king to the banquet. That banquet was evidently postponed in order for Haman to carry out the command of the king. Since such an event would be known to everyone in the palace, Esther must have heard about it. Perhaps she and her ladies saw the whole procession.

"Then said his wise men and Zeresh his wife unto him, If Mordecai be the seed of the Jews, before whom thou hast begun to fall, thou shalt not prevail against him, but shalt surely fall before him." Since they must have previously known that Mordecai was a Jew, it seems strange that they did not say anything about this before. People may be aware of certain things and yet not be affected by them until something unusual takes place. Then suddenly their attitude changes. The same ones who urged the hanging of Mordecai now declare that he is invincible. They do not even try to encourage Haman to believe that matters might turn out better than he had anticipated. They prophesied nothing but gloom. Haman had begun to fall and nothing could now prevent his complete undoing. Such talk is characteristic of Satan and his agents. Initially they are ready with advice which promises complete success. But when their poor dupes discover their doom, they have no message of comfort, only one of despair.

Perhaps this message is being read by one to whom Satan has promised much. You may already realize that you are doomed to disappointment. He did the same with Adam and Eve in the Garden of Eden. He promised that if they ate the forbidden fruit they would be as gods. But when they stood before Him, whose one commandment they had disobeyed, Satan had no word of comfort for them. Only in the "good news" of the Gospel do we hear words of hope and salvation that every poor lost sinner needs. But Haman's friends had no such words for him.

"And while they were yet talking with him, came the king's chamberlains, and hasted to bring Haman unto the banquet that Esther had prepared." That was to be his last banquet. If he had waited for the chamberlains to bring him the day before, the whole story might have been different. Meanwhile the Lord had worked out His plans and purposes. Satan may be wise, but he is not omniscient. Had he known the way things would turn out, he might have advised his poor slave differently.

Haman had begun to fall, not only before Mordecai, but before the Lord who "is known by the judgment which he executeth; the wicked is snared in the work of his own hands," Psa. 9:16. It is "a fearful thing to fall into the hands of the living God," Heb. 10:31. The story of Haman's downfall should be a warning to all who imagine that they can defeat Him. However we can take comfort from the study of this chapter when we consider the wonderful way in which the Lord vindicates His own who trust in Him. Perhaps as in the case of Mordecai, our faith is not even articulate. But God hears the groaning which cannot be uttered. He is able to do exceeding abundantly above all that we ask (audibly) or think (inaudibly).

CHAPTER SEVEN — The Second Banquet

■ IN CHAPTER 5 Queen Esther manifested much self-restraint when she did not present her real request at the first banquet. There are a number of references in the Old Testament which show that the Lord Himself waited until "the second time" to make known His real reason for speaking to His own. "The angel of the Lord called unto Abraham out of heaven the second time" after he had offered up Isaac as the Lord commanded him. It was then that He said, "In blessing I will bless thee, and in multiplying I will mutiply thy seed as the stars of heaven, and as the sand which is upon the sea shore; and thy seed shall possess the gate of his enemies; and in thy seed shall all the nations of the earth be blessed; because thou hast obeyed my voice," Gen. 22:17, 18.

When the Lord spoke to Abraham the first time, "the scripture, foreseeing that God would justify the heathen through faith, preached before the gospel unto Abraham, saying, In thee shall all nations be blessed," Gal. 3:8. But when He spoke to him the second time, He made mention of the Seed "which is Christ," verse 16. In direct connection He also said, "And thy seed shall possess the gate of his enemies." It may be that Queen Esther had that promise in mind when she approached her heathen husband with her request.

"So the king and Haman came to banquet with Esther the queen. And the king said again unto Esther on the second day at the banquet of wine, What is thy petition, queen Esther? and it shall be granted thee: and what is thy request? and it shall be performed, even to the half of the kingdom." Once again it is the king who takes the initiative. He is more personal than he was when he made a similar offer at the first banquet. Here he actually addresses her as "queen Esther." It recalls the fact that when our blessed Lord called Mary by name that she recognized Him as her Lord and Master, John 20:16. But the Good Shepherd "calleth his own sheep by name," John 10:3. We all know the thrill of being personally recognized by others.

In addressing her as "queen Esther," the king was giving emphasis to her royal position. Since she was about to make a crucial request, this must have been encouraging. She was not only coming to a king, she was coming to him as a queen.

"Then Esther the queen answered and said, If I have found favor in thy sight, O king, and if it please the king, let my life be given me at my *petition*, and my people at my *request*." She took the king literally. That is why she repeated the very words which he used when he offered to give her her heart's desire. The word *petition* comes from a root which means "to inquire" as if to ascertain the will and pleasure of the one to whom the petition is addressed. It also has in it the idea of demanding. The word *request* comes from a root which means "to search out, or strive after." That reminds us of the man who was granted his request "because of his importunity," Luke 11:8. It also reminds us of the Apostle Paul who wrote to the Romans, "I beseech you, brethren, for the Lord Jesus Christ's sake, and for the love of the Spirit, that ye *strive* together with me in your prayers to God for me; that I may be delivered from them that do not believe," Rom. 15:30. Basically prayer is a matter of ascertaining the will of the Lord and then earnestly beseeching Him to grant that which is according to His will.

The reason for Queen Esther's earnestness is clearly seen in what follows. She and her people had been sold "to be destroyed, to be slain, and to perish." In saying that she was using the words of the document which had been written by the king's scribes, sealed with the king's seal and carried to the remotest corners of the Persian Empire by posts who were "hastened by the king's commandment," Esther 3:13, 15. In saying "we are sold," she was referring to Haman's offer of ten thousand talents of silver "to bring it into the king's treasuries."

"But," she continued, "if we had been sold for bondmen and bondwomen, I had held my tongue, although the enemy could not countervail [or, compensate for] the king's damage." Evidently the Jews, even though they were a captive people at that time, were not looked upon as slaves. Presumably they had all of the privileges of free man and women. Esther indicates that they might have accepted a change of social status without protest. But such a change, she intimates, would not be for the king's advantage. The money which Haman had promised to pay into the king's treasuries would not compensate for the loss to the king.

There is much food for thought in that statement. The service of a slave can never be the same in value as that of a free man. Repeatedly the Apostle Paul referred to himself as a slave of the Lord Jesus Christ. But that was voluntary slavery, like that of the Hebrew who had the opportunity to be free, but preferred perpetual servitude because of love for his master, his wife and his children, Exod. 21:2-6. The slavery to which Queen Esther referred was not after that order. Nor was that all that Haman desired. His purpose was not only to enslave the Jews but ultimately to exterminate them.

"Then the king Ahasuerus answered and said unto Esther the queen, Who is he, and where is he, that durst presume in his heart to do so?" Had she followed the course of Nathan when he came to charge

David with the crime of having murdered Uriah the Hittite she would have said, "Thou art the man," II Sam. 12:7. But she did not use that method.

"And Esther said, The adversary and enemy is this wicked Haman." Before she mentioned his name, she used three strong words to describe him. To begin with, he is "the adversary," a type of him who is our "adversary the devil," and who, "as a roaring lion, walketh about, seeking whom he may devour," I Peter 5:8. He is also the "enemy," or one who hates the people of God. And as the "wicked one" he is the very antithesis of goodness. This last epithet in the New Testament describes both Satan and the Antichrist, I John 2:13 and II Thess. 2:8.

"Then Haman was afraid before the king and the queen." In one fell stroke Esther had exposed the character of him who dined that day with the royal couple. She also had answered the king's double question, "Who is he, and where is he, that durst presume in his heart to do so?" He was there in the palace. He had walked right into the trap from which there was now no escape.

The king was infuriated! Rising from the banquet of wine in his wrath he went into the palace garden. He must have realized that he was involved in the plot to destroy his wife's people even though he may have been led into it innocently. For a man in his position to be deceived must have been humiliating indeed. It seems strange that he did not know until then that Esther was a Jewess. The discovery of that fact would certainly put him in a dilemma. He must have been thoroughly convinced that all Esther had charged was true, because he did not ask her to prove her statement. In her heart-moving plea for her life Esther had used the very terminology of the document dictated by the despicable Haman.

In the meantime "Haman stood up to make request for his life to Esther the queen; for he saw that there was evil determined against him by the king." He made no attempt to explain. Neither did he express any sorrow for what he had done. It was his own life that he was concerned about. He did not even go as far as Judas did when he said, "I have sinned in that I have betrayed the innocent blood," Matt. 27:4. Probably he had seen Ahasuerus in a fit of anger before. But this rage would not subside after a brief interlude in the garden.

Apparently Esther remained silent through all of this. Her case was now in the hands of the king. We read of no display of emotion on her part. If Haman thought that he could play on her sympathies and emotions, he was mistaken. All too soon, so far as he was concerned, "the king returned out of the palace garden into the place of the banquet of wine." What he saw when he returned only made matters worse. "Haman was fallen upon the bed whereon Esther was." Beside himself in his desperation when he realized that his own life was in jeopardy, the one who had so boldly planned the extermination of a race of people became a coward in the face of death.

The "bed whereon Esther was," was probably one "of gold and silver," mentioned in Esther 1:6. The Orientals did not sit at a table as we do now. They reclined as did our Lord and His disciples at the Last Supper. That will explain the presence of a "bed" in the banqueting house. Nevertheless the king misinterpreted Haman's actions, for he said, "Will he force the queen also before me in the house?"

However unjust this remark of Ahasuerus was, it had its due effect upon the servants standing by. "As the word went out of the king's mouth, they covered Haman's face." Apparently Haman had no friend in the court. Not one rose to plead his case or even to suggest to the enraged monarch that his judgment was harsh. The covering of Haman's face was the sign that he was doomed to die even though the king had not yet pronounced the death sentence upon him.

It is at this point in the story that we learn of the presence of others in the banqueting house. Among these was Harbonah, one of "the seven chamberlains that served in the presence of Ahasuerus the king," Esther 1:10. He was one of the group which was sent to bring in Queen Vashti to show the people and the princes her beauty. But this time he was about a different kind of business. He knew about "the gallows fifty cubits high, which Haman had made for Mordecai, who had spoken good for the king." He did no more than call attention to it, but that was all that was needed. The fact that he mentioned Mordecai as the one for whom the gallows were being erected was also significant. Harbonah was supplying information which Queen Esther might have used when she was pleading for her own life and for the lives of her people.

Haman did not get a trial by a jury of his peers. Neither were any other witnesses called. Esther had described him for what he was. Harbonah revealed the fact that Haman had planned to kill Mordecai before the date set by the decree to exterminate the Jews. But what he had planned for another, and that an innocent man, turned out to be the means of his own doom. When the king heard of the gallows which he had prepared for Mordecai, he thundered out, "Hang him thereon!" Thus Haman fell into the very pit which he had dug for another. How true is the proverb, "Whoso diggeth a pit shall fall therein: and he that rolleth a stone, it will return upon him," Prov. 26:27! "For he shall have judgment without mercy, that hath showed no mercy," James 2:13.

It is interesting to find that the word here used for *gallows* in the Greek translation of the passage is the same word which is used for the cross of our Lord Jesus Christ in the Greek New Testament in such passages as Acts 5:30; 10:39; and 13:29. It is also found in Galatians 3:13 and I Peter 2:24. The word *tree* in all of these passages refers to the cross on which our Lord Jesus was crucified. But the same word is also used in Revelation 2:7 and 22:2, 14 in connection with "the tree of life." Like Haman, we deserved to die that death of shame and loss. But the Lord Jesus died there in our place as our Substitute. And thus the cross, or the tree, which was a curse for Him becomes for us "the tree of life."

"Then was the king's wrath pacified." It subsided like the waters of a flood subside. But the death of Christ did something more for us than to cause the wrath of God to subside. By means of that cross He "delivered us from the wrath to come." I Thess. 1:10. And because of that we have peace with God through our Lord Jesus Christ. Haman's plea for his life was silenced when they covered his face and took him to his own home to die. That brings to mind the words of the Psalmist who said, "I have seen the wicked in great power, and spreading himself like a green bay tree. Yet he passed away, and, lo, he was not: yea, I sought him, but he could not be found. Mark the perfect man, and behold the upright: for the end of that man is peace," Psa. 37:35-37.

CHAPTER EIGHT
A Passion for Souls

■ ONE OF THE FIRST evidences of a genuine conversion is the desire that others may share in "so great salvation." This is often referred to as a "passion for souls," and it is just that. Some Christians retain it only for a little while after their conversion. In others it grows stronger as they grow older in the faith. But most of us need to have this holy fire kindled afresh. Let us pray that the Holy Spirit who inspired this chapter will stir us all to greater zeal in seeking the salvation of others.

In the previous chapter Queen Esther was pleading for her own life and the lives of her people. She was concerned with more then her own personal safety. Such is the grace of Him who is "able to do exceeding abundantly above all that we ask or think," Eph. 3:20. Esther's deliverance was assured when the king ordered the execution of Haman. But nothing was said about her people. She may have thought that their safety was implied, but she was taking nothing for granted. Nor was she less concerned about them even though she herself was safe. Her example could put many of us to shame. How many never give a moment's thought to the salvation of others! They seem content that they themselves have been saved. But Esther was like Rahab, who made the two spies who came to Jericho swear unto her by the Lord that they would also show kindness unto her father's house and deliver their lives from death, Josh. 2:12, 13. In like manner Esther planned for the deliverance of her people.

"On that day did the king Ahasuerus give the house of Haman the Jews' enemy unto Esther the queen." Shortly before this Haman had "called for his friends, and Zeresh his wife. And Haman told them of the glory of his riches, and the multitude of his children," Esther 5:10, 11. Now all of this was committed unto Esther to do with as she pleased. All the members of that household were her servants from that day forward. An illustration of this is the case of Mephibosheth to whom King David gave "all that pertained to Saul and to his house." That included the servants, because Ziba and his sons were to till the land for Mephibosheth and to bring in the fruits in order that he might lack nothing. "Ziba had fifteen sons and twenty servants," II Sam. 9:9, 10. According to Esther 9, Haman had ten sons, all of whom were slain shortly after this.

Although this was now hers, Esther decides to put everything into the hands of Mordecai. And so "Mordecai came before the king; for Esther had told what he was unto her." Not only had Haman's plot compelled Esther to reveal her identity, but now she identifies with the one whom Haman had intended to hang. These are some of the blessed fruits of persecution! When God's people are at ease, they tend to drift apart. But in times of persecution they learn to value each other. The means by which the enemy hopes to scatter them God uses to draw them closer together. That is why the Apostle Paul could actually glory in tribulation. Thus that which we are apt to call a calamity becomes a blessing.

Without a moment's hesitation "the king took off his ring, which he had taken from Haman, and gave it unto Mordecai." It was a sad day for the Jews when Ahasuerus gave that ring to Haman because the document which authorized their extermination was sealed with it. The surrender of the ring was probably the last thing which Haman did in the presence of the king. And the conferring of the ring upon Mordecai seems to have been the signal for Esther to "set Mordecai over the house of Haman."

Esther's giving this power to Mordecai points to a beautiful lesson. Vengeance must be taken, but she committed that into the hands of another, as the word of God exhorts us to do. It is written, "Vengeance is mine; I will repay, saith the Lord," Rom. 12:19. In referring to the enemies of His people, the Lord said, "To me belongeth vengeance, and recompense; their foot shall slide in due time: for the day of their calamity is at hand, and the things that shall come upon them make haste. For the Lord shall judge his people, and repent himself for his servants, when he seeth that their power is gone, and there is none shut up, or left," Deut. 32:35, 36. Perhaps Queen Esther had those verses in mind when she gave the house of Haman to Mordecai.

But still she must provide for the deliverance of her people. And so she "spake yet again before the king, and fell down at his feet, and besought him with tears to put away the mischief of Haman the Agagite, and his device that he had devised against the Jews." Haman was no more, but the evil he had done continued after him. Judicially Satan also has been judged and cast out. In anticipation of His glorious victory over Satan, our Lord could say, "Now is the judgment of this world: now shall the prince of this world be cast out," John 12:31. But his evil devices are still with us. It should move us to tears as we think of the souls whom he controls.

Esther did not shed tears when she pled for her own life. Of course she may not have realized all that she had been saved from. How many of us realized at the time of our conversion all that the Lord had done for us? But as we grow in grace and in the knowledge of our Lord and Savior, we become better acquainted with Him and His Word. In the process we also learn something of the awful predicament that was ours when we were in our sins and under the wrath of God. When we reflect on the plight of the unsaved, we are moved to go forth to snatch them as brands from the burning. If the unsaved were conscious of their present peril, many of them would lose no time in coming to the Savior. And if Christians truly believed this, there would be more weeping over lost souls, even as the Lord Jesus wept over the city of Jerusalem, Luke 19:41.

Queen Esther's earnestness caused the king to hold out the golden scepter toward her. "So Esther arose, and stood before the king." Encouraged by this gesture of grace, she rose from her knees to speak on behalf of her people. In her plea there is no reference to the house of Haman. It is the safety of her people that is paramount. The punishment of the house of Haman will be considered later. So she said, "If it please the king, and if I have found favor in his sight, and the thing seem right before the king, and I be pleasing in his eyes, let it be written to reverse the letters devised by Haman the son of Hammedatha the Agagite, which he wrote to destroy the Jews which are in all the king's provinces." She was careful to consider both his pleasure and his honor. In like manner we should come to the King of kings with our petitions!

Of course she did not hide her own feelings. But she expressed how deeply moved she was, "How can I endure to see the evil that shall come unto my people? or how can I endure to see the destruction of my kindred?" She could not bear the thought of it, much less the sight of it. How much are we affected by the future destiny of the lost? Esther's feelings were bound up in love for her people. Oh, that we loved men enough to weep over them and to plead for them at the throne of Him who is not willing that any should perish but that all should come to repentance!

In his reply to the eloquent plea of Esther, Ahasuerus reminded her and Mordecai that he had already given the house of Haman to Esther and that Haman had been hanged on the gallows "because he laid his hand upon the Jews." It seems that the immediate reason for the execution of Haman was that the king found him "fallen upon the bed whereon Esther was." Here, however, the king made it appear that it was because Haman had laid his hand upon the Jews.

It is interesting to compare what Ahasuerus said to Esther and Mordecai with what he said to Haman when he gave him permission to write the document of destruction. To Haman he said, "The silver is given thee, the people also, to do with them as it seemeth good unto thee." But to Esther and Mordecai he said, "Write ye also for the Jews, as it liketh you, in the king's name, and seal it with the king's ring: for the writing which is written in the king's name, and sealed with the king's ring, may no man reverse." Can it be that this time he made it emphatic that his own heart was in the matter? He clearly does not expect to reverse what Esther and Mordecai are about to do. The previous order was supposedly irrevocable, but still it was only the word of a man.

We who trust in the living God have something far better than that. "Men verily swear by the greater: and an oath for confirmation is to them an end of all strife. Wherein God, willing more abundantly to show unto the heirs of promise the immutability of his counsel, confirmed it by an oath: that by two immutable things, in which it was impossible for God to lie, we might have strong consolation, who have fled for refuge to lay hold upon the hope set before us: which hope we have as an anchor of the soul, both sure and steadfast," Heb. 6:16-19. Esther and Mordecai had the king's name and the king's ring. But we have two better things—God's Word and God's oath.

How firm a foundation, ye saints of the Lord,
Is laid for your faith in His excellent word!
What more can He say, than to you He hath said,—
To you, who for refuge to Jesus have fled?

"Then were the king's scribes called at that time in the third month, that is, the month Sivan, on the three and twentieth day thereof." This third month was the third month of the Jewish sacred year, extending from the moon of our month of May to the new moon of the month of June. This must not be confused with the third month of the Jewish civil year which roughly corresponds to the latter part of November and the first part of December. The third month of the sacred year was the month in which the Jews celebrated the Feast of Weeks, known as Pentecost. According to Deuteronomy 16:9-12, the Israelite was to number "seven weeks from such time as thou beginnest to put the sickle to the corn. And thou shalt keep the feast of weeks unto the Lord thy God with a tribute of a free-will offering of thine hand, which thou shalt give unto the Lord thy God, according as the Lord thy God hath blessed thee: and thou shalt rejoice before the Lord thy God... and thou shalt remember that thou wast a bondman in Egypt."

In Leviticus 23:16 this same time is referred to as "fifty days" at the close of which they were to offer "a new meat [or meal] offering unto the Lord." In view of what happened at Pentecost after the Lord Jesus ascended to Heaven, it is not difficult to see the prophetic significance in this. Mordecai had said that if Esther were to keep silent at that time "then shall enlargement and deliverance arise to the Jews from another place." In saying that he spoke more than what he knew. Deliverance came from Heaven, not from any earthly source. It came at the time set by Him who has put the times and the seasons in His own power, Acts 1:7.

Apparently the wording of the new decree was left entirely to Mordecai, for "it was written according to all that Mordecai commanded unto the Jews, and to the lieutenants, and the deputies and rulers of the provinces which are from India unto Ethiopia, an hundred twenty and seven provinces, unto every province according to the writing thereof, and unto every people after their language, and to the Jews according to their writing and according to their language." Everyone would know that the Jews were allowed to defend themselves.

The fact that it was to be published just as extensively as the former decree is suggestive of the Gospel. "The soul that sinneth, it shall die" is universal in its scope, because all have sinned and come short of the glory of God. But the good news of the Gospel is also universal in its scope "for God so loved the world, that he gave his only begotten Son, that whosoever believeth in him should not perish, but have everlasting life," John 3:16.

The decree sent out by Mordecai gave the Jews the right to defend themselves against their enemies. The Christian also has the right to defend himself in his conflict with the Devil and his hosts. Unlike the Jews of Esther's day, "we wrestle not against flesh and blood, but against principalities, against powers, against the rulers of the darkness of this world, against spiritual wickedness [or wicked spirits] in high places." These are the hosts of Satan who is the prince of the power of the air. Every Christian must be aware of this opposition even though he may not always be able to identify it. Satan may use human instruments to accomplish his ends. Behind Haman was Satan whose desire it has been from the very beginning to destroy the children of God. The culmination of his bloody trail is seen in the crucifixion of our Lord. Every martyr who has sealed his testimony with his blood is in this noble succession.

But Satan is wise enough to know that "the blood of the martyrs is the seed of the church." Therefore he prefers at times to wage a "cold war" to slowly wear out the saints. For this reason we are exhorted to put on the whole armor of God so that we may be able to stand in the evil day; having our loins girt about with truth, and having on the breastplate of righteousness, our feet shod with the preparation of the Gospel of peace; and above all taking the shield of faith wherewith we shall be able to quench all the fiery darts of the wicked one. For our peace of mind we are to have our head covered with the helmet of salvation. But for offensive warfare we are to take the sword of the Spirit, which is the word of God: praying with all prayer and supplication in the spirit, Eph. 6:10-18.

Such protection is provided all children of God who will avail themselves of it. This chapter furnishes a good illustration of that. Mordecai "wrote in the king Ahasuerus' name, and sealed it with the king's ring, and sent letters by posts on horseback, and riders on mules, camels, and young dromedaries: wherein the king granted the Jews which were *in every city* to gather themselves together, and to stand for their life, to destroy, to slay, and to cause to perish, all the power of the people and province that would assault them, both little ones and women, and to take spoil of them for a prey." If we look upon "the power of the people" as a type of Satan which is arrayed against us, we shall have no difficulty in making the application.

The Jews were to *gather together* and they were to stand. They were to present a united front against their common foe. Likewise we gather together as the Lord's people for prayer. We then come into combat with the hosts of wickedness. But many of God's children know little about such warfare. Such conflict requires spiritual energy from feeding on the Word of God. Then when we gather together to pray, we shall be able to stand. The glorious result will be victories of faith "in the Lord and in the power of his might."

This chapter mentions "spoil." Paul tells us, by

the Spirit, that our Lord Jesus "spoiled principalities and powers" when He "made a show of them openly, triumphing over them," Col. 2:15. This refers to our Lord's victory over death and over him who had the might of death, the Devil. Our Lord was victorious over death when He rose from the dead. But His triumph is seen in His ascension to Heaven, for then He went through the domain of Satan, the prince of the power of the air. Thus He opened the way for us to come boldly unto the throne of grace so that we may triumph in His triumphs. Because He poured out His soul unto death it was promised Him that He shall divide the spoil with the strong, Isa. 53:12.

Another detail in this chapter reminds us of Ephesians 6. "Upon *one day* in all of the provinces of king Ahasuerus, namely, upon the thirteenth *day* of the twelfth month, which is the month Adar. The copy of the writing for a commandment to be given in every province was published unto all people, and that the Jews should be ready against *that day* to avenge themselves on their enemies." Christians are told to put on the whole armor of God that they may be "able to withstand in the *evil day*." But over all this is the One who has put the times and the seasons in His own power. He knows how to deliver the godly out of his trials and from the share of the enemy. Therefore no day which the enemy may set for our destruction need take us by surprise.

"So the posts that rode upon mules and camels went out, being hastened and pressed on by the king's commandment. And the decree was given at Shushan the palace." There was no time to be lost. If the enemy can get us to put off prayer or anything else that might result in victory, he can defeat us.

It was not only an exhortation that was sent out that day. It was something more than permission to defend themselves which was granted to the Jews; it was "the king's commandment." And what if some "post" or messenger, directed to go to some remote province, had chosen to delay until *the day* had passed! The consequences would have been serious. We, too, have been sent forth with an urgent message. We also live in an evil day. Let us then be on our way and those to whom we have been sent with the King's commandment shall hear the message of His grace before it is forever too late.

The fact that this message was "given at Shushan the palace" gave it royal dignity and importance which brought honor to those chosen to deliver it. Those "posts" were really the king's ambassadors. The content of their message should have made them even more eager to deliver it. Then, too, such a message was found to find a glorious reception by the Jews, not only because they could defend themselves, but also because royal authority guaranteed the reliability of it. Likewise the messenger of the good news is a royal ambassador. Those to whom the message is addressed can rely upon it, because it is backed up by the power and authority of the King of kings. In the preamble of the Great Commission our Lord Jesus said, "All power is given unto me in heaven and in earth. Go ye therefore..." Matt. 28:18, 19.

Mordecai went out "from the presence of the king in royal apparel of blue and white, and with a great crown of gold, and with a garment of fine linen and purple." "A dress of blue and white was held in great estimation among the Persians: so that Mordecai, whom the king delighted to honor, was in fact arrayed in the royal dress and insignia. The variety and the kind of insignia worn by a favorite at once makes known to the people the particular dignity to which he has been raised," *Jamieson, Fausset and Brown*.

But long before the Persian era the Lord had said, "Speak unto the children of Israel, and bid them that they make them fringes in the borders of their garments throughout their generations, and that they put upon the fringe of the borders a ribband of blue: and it shall be unto you for a fringe, that ye may look upon it, and remember all the commandments of the Lord and do them; and that ye seek not after your own heart and your own eyes," Num. 15:38, 39. Thus we can see that blue would also have a spiritual significance for the intelligent Israelite.

There are two different words used for crown in the original language of the book of Esther. The one here used differs from that used to describe the crown worn by Queen Vashti, and later by Queen Esther. The word here used in the Hebrew is the same as that of which we have the verb form in Psalm 8:5, in which we get a preview of our Lord crowned with glory and honor. "The garment of fine linen and purple" seems to have been an outer garment. The fine linen, as we know from Revelation 19:8, is symbolic of righteousness, and purple is the symbol of royalty. Mordecai's distinction certainly excelled that with which Haman was compelled to array him in chapter 6.

All of this met with popular approval. "The city of Shushan rejoiced and was glad." Shortly before that same city "was perplexed," Esther 3:15. "The Jews had light, and gladness, and joy, and honor." Even before their actual deliverance they could rejoice in it. That is after the manner of faith. It enables one to look into the future with calm and certainty, knowing that what God promises He is able to perform, Rom. 4:21.

Verse 16 of the present chapter reminds us of Psalm 97:10-12 where we read that the Lord "preserveth the souls of his saints; he delivereth them out of the hand of the wicked. *Light* is sown for the righteous, and *gladness* for the upright in heart. *Rejoice* in the Lord, ye righteous; and give thanks at the remembrance of his holiness." The Jews of Esther's day could truly prove the truth of those words. In place of the darkness, the sorrow, the grief and the dishonor which had been theirs, they could rejoice in the four-fold blessing of the Lord.

This blessing was not limited to the city of Shushan. "In every province, and in every city, whithersoever the king's commandment and his decree came, the Jews had joy and gladness, a feast and a good day." The original word for *feast* in this verse occurs more often in the book of Esther than in any other book of the Old Testament. It is also translated banquet in chapters 5, 6 and 7. It is first used in the Bible to describe the feast which Lot prepared for the angels who visited him, Gen. 19:3. It is also used to describe the great feast which Abraham made "the same day that Isaac was weaned." Since it is not used in Leviticus 23, it was not a religious feast. Later, however, it became a national feast for the Jews.

The effect of the new decree upon the people of the land was remarkable. "Many of the people of the land became Jews; for the fear of the Jews fell upon them." The motive which impelled them to become proselytes seems based more on the fear of the Jews than the fear of the Lord. That which is done for fear of man is apt to change. It is the fear of the Lord, not the fear of man, which is the beginning of wisdom.

CHAPTER NINE 1-19 *The Tables Turned*

■ THERE IS NO SUCH THING as "chance" in the plan and purpose of God, even though Haman did cast lots to determine the day on which he hoped to destroy the Jews. We have seen already that the lot is cast into the lap, but the whole disposing thereof is of the Lord, Prov. 16:33. What may appear to be a matter of luck, or chance, is really a part of God's divine purpose.

The favorable turn in the affairs of the Jews was preceded by great honor bestowed upon Mordecai. But such honor is not something to be enjoyed as a matter of personal advantage. In this chapter we see how Mordecai used his high position for the good and blessing of others.

The fateful day "when the king's commandment and his decree drew near to be put in execution" arrived. That was the day when "the enemies of the Jews hoped to have power over them." How excited everybody must have been. Twelve long months had passed since that date was set, not because it would take that long to make preparation, but because Haman had found it difficult to determine "the lucky day." Since it was so difficult to fix the day that they "hoped to have power over" the Jews, apparently there was doubt about the final outcome.

The original word for *power* in this verse is the same as that which is translated *rule* in the next sentence. The Psalmist used the same word in Psalm 119:133 when he prayed, "Order my steps in thy word: and let not any iniquity *have dominion* over me." The answer to that prayer is found in Romans 6:14 where the Apostle Paul tells us by the Spirit that "sin shall not have dominion over you: for ye are not under the law, but under grace." Naturally the Jews of that day had no such knowledge, but we know that the things which happened to them were written for our benefit. Thus we may learn how the Lord delivered His own from the power and dominion of sin and Satan when "it was turned to the contrary" and "the Jews had rule over them that hated them."

The Jews first gathered "themselves together in their cities throughout all the provinces of the king Ahasuerus, to lay hand on such as sought their hurt." It would appear from this statement that they had had certain cities assigned to them by the king by gathering in their own cities, they would not provoke hostility by going where they did not belong. In that they showed more common sense than do some of God's children today. Many Christians are caught in the bonds of sin and Satan, because they insist on going where they have no need to go. Then failure to gather with their brethren is often the first step on the downward road of backsliding. The happy man is "the man that walketh not in the counsel of the ungodly, nor standeth in the way of sinners, nor sitteth in the seat of the scornful," Psa. 1:1.

If the enemy decides to pursue us even in the place of God's choosing, then he exposes himself to danger and defeat. There may be times when we must meet the enemy on his own ground. But it is safer to meet him where we may be certain of the complete protection of God. Then it will be true of us as it was of them in that day, "no man could withstand them; for the fear of them fell upon all the people." "Whatsoever is born of God overcometh the world, and this is the victory, that overcometh the world, even our faith," I John 5:4.

The Jews also were helped by the officers of King Ahasuerus, "because the fear of Mordecai fell upon them. For Mordecai was great in the king's house, and his fame went out throughout all the provinces: for this man Mordecai waxed greater and greater," like King David who "waxed greater and greater: for the Lord of hosts was with him," I Chron. 11:9. Possibly Mordecai is a type of the Lord Jesus of whom John the Baptist said, "He must increase but I must decrease," John 3:30. Mordecai evidently went on "increasing" to the end of his life. Truly "the path of the just is as the shining light that shineth more and more unto the perfect day," Prov. 4:18.

Under such powerful leadership the Jews fared well. "Thus the Jews smote all their enemies with the stroke of the sword, and slaughter, and destruction, and did what they would unto those that hated them." Christians also fight, but we do not fight according to the flesh. The weapons of our warfare are not carnal, but mighty through God to the pulling down of strongholds, II Cor. 10:4.

One of our mightiest weapons is "the sword of

the Spirit," Eph. 6:17. From the context of Ephesians 6 the sword of the Spirit is a weapon for a special kind of warfare. Because it is called "the word of God," some believe that whenever we use the word of God we are handling a sword. But the expression does not refer to the Bible as a whole. A more accurate translation reads, "the saying of God," which refers to a particular text which we may use against the host of wicked spirits. This cannot refer to a warfare with human beings, because the text says that we do not wrestle against flesh and blood.

If we regard Haman as a type of the Devil, and his sons and servants as types of those hosts which are under the leadership of the Devil, we can make an application for our own instruction and encouragement. The fact that "in Shushan the palace the Jews slew and destroyed five hundred men" lends itself well to such an application. Those slain must have identified themselves as enemies of the Jews, because the Jews only attacked their enemies.

Among those slain in the palace we find the ten sons of Haman, all of whom are mentioned by name. Thomas Newberry has ventured to give the meanings of the names in the margin of *The Englishman's Bible*. There we are told that Parshandatha means "of noble birth"; Dalphon, "strenuous"; Aspatha, "given by the horse"; Poratha, "ornament"; Aridatha, "great birth"; Parmashta, "strongfisted"; Arisai, "like to a lion"; and Vayzatha, "sincere." He offers no meanings for Adalia and Aridai. This was a proud family. The ten sons of Haman must have taken the lead in an attempt to carry out the decree of their father. But not one of them lived to carry on his father's name.

The historian notes that the Jews did not touch

the spoil. In this they showed more self-control than Achan of whom we read in the book of Joshua. Among the spoils of Jericho he saw a costly garment, two hundred shekels of silver and a wedge of gold. He could not resist the temptation to carry them off. But the Jews at Shushan the palace were not interested in material things. There were greater things at stake than silver and gold. They did not allow that which was material and secondary to take their eyes off the real objective. Their existence as a people meant more to them than temporary riches. We, too, should exhibit such a fine sense of values.

We now come to the report which was made to the king. "On that day the number of those that were slain in Shushan the palace was brought before the king. And the king said unto Esther the queen, The Jews have slain and destroyed five hundred men in Shushan the palace, and the ten sons of Haman; what have they done in the rest of the king's provinces? now what is thy petition? and it shall be granted thee: or what is thy request further? and it shall be done." Apparently the king expressed no surprise at the large number of anti-Semites which had been slain in his palace. The report from the provinces had not yet come in. But whether the number be large or small, he stands ready to grant the queen even more than she had already received from him, for he states, "it shall be granted," and "it shall be done."

"Then said queen Esther, If it please the king, let it be granted to the Jews which are in Shushan the palace to do tomorrow also according unto this day's decree, and let Haman's ten sons be hanged upon the gallows." The queen showed that she was aware that the decree of Ahasuerus had specified that the Jews should be ready against that day, that is, the thirteenth day of the twelfth month. The decree did not go beyond that one day, but she must have known that other enemies had not yet been apprehended. They may have gone into hiding when they saw what took place. To allow them to live would be to risk future assaults. They must be completely exterminated.

"And the king commanded it so to be done: and the decree was given at Shushan; and they hanged Haman's ten sons." We know from II Samuel 21:12 that the corpses of those who had been slain were sometimes hanged afterward to expose them to open shame. For example, "the bones of Saul and the bones of Jonathan his son" were stolen by the men of Jabesh-gilead, "from the street of Beth-shan, where the Philistines had hanged them. Such was probably the case here. Queen Esther would never have requested such a thing without great provocation. If we knew all that was involved in the plot of Haman, we would probably find that her request was fully justified, for she was neither a Jezebel nor an Athaliah.

Royal permission having been obtained for another day of vengeance "the Jews that were in Shushan gathered themselves together on the fourteenth day also of the month Adar, and slew three hundred men at Shushan; but on the prey they laid not their hand." If those three hundred men had been permitted to live, they would have been a constant threat. When God commissioned King Saul to "go and utterly destroy the sinners the Amalekites, and fight against them until they be consumed," he and his people spared Agag the king of the Amalekites, "and the best of the sheep, and of the oxen, and of the fatlings, and the lambs, and all that was good, and would not utterly destroy them: but every thing that was vile and refuse, that they destroyed utterly," I Sam. 15:9 ff. This failure to carry out the commandment of the Lord led to Saul's rejection as king of Israel. He had to learn through bitter experience that "to obey is better than sacrifice, and to hearken than the fat of rams," verse 22. The Jews of Esther's day did not make that mistake.

If the anti-Semites of Esther's day were Amalekites, then it may be that the Jews remembered that the Lord had said to Moses, "Write this for a memorial in a book, and rehearse it in the ears of Joshua: for I will utterly put out the remembrance of Amalek from under heaven," Exod. 17:14. That the Jews were to be the divine instruments to accomplish this is clear from the words of Moses in Deuteronomy 25:17-19. "Remember what Amalek did unto thee by the way, when ye were come forth out of Egypt; how he met thee by the way, and smote the hindmost of thee, even all that were feeble behind thee, when thou wast faint and weary; and he feared not God. Therefore it shall be, when the Lord thy God hath given thee rest from all thine enemies round about, in the land which the Lord thy God giveth thee for an inheritance to possess it, that thou shalt blot out the remembrance of Amalek from under heaven; thou shalt not forget it." Had they done that after they were settled in the land, Haman and his house would never have been heard of. Their very existence proved that Israel had failed to carry out this commandment of the Lord. Their present plight was the fruit of their disobedience. That may explain the thoroughness with which they went about their destruction now.

"But the other Jews that were in the king's provinces, gathered themselves together, and stood for their lives, and had rest from their enemies, and slew of their foes seventy and five thousand, but they laid not their hands on the prey." The number of casualties in what was really a defensive action by the Jews proves the magnitude of the plot to exterminate them. If they had not "gathered themselves together, and stood for their lives," the final outcome would have been defeat instead of victory and "rest from their enemies." We have already seen the importance of gathering and standing—two examples which the Church of our day might well heed. Nothing weakens like division and the enemy knows that. Let us not fail then to learn the lesson from this part of God's Word which will enable us to gain victories over our adversary.

The Jews that were in the king's provinces required only one day to dispose of their enemies. That was "on the thirteenth day of the month Adar; and the fourteenth day of the same rested they, and made it a day of feasting and gladness." The fact that they rested on the fourteenth day implies that they kept the day as a sabbath. If so, it was not a sabbath of sadness but of gladness and feasting. It was the Lord's plan that the sabbath should be a day of refreshing and rest. "Six days shalt thou do thy work, and on the seventh thou shalt rest: that thine ox and thine ass may rest, and the son of thy handmaid, and the stranger, may be refreshed," Exod. 23:12.

"But the Jews that were at Shushan assembled together on the thirteenth day thereof, and on the fourteenth thereof; and on the fifteenth day of the same they rested, and made it a day of feasting and gladness." Probably it was a day of thanksgiving to Him who had given them this great deliverance. If the fourteenth day was a sabbath, then this fifteenth day would be the first day of a new week.

The difference between "the Jews that were in Shushan" and "the Jews of the villages, that dwell in unwalled towns" may illustrate that some of the children of God seem to realize and enjoy their deliverance from sin and Satan sooner than others. With some, the joy of being set "free from the law of sin and death," Rom. 8:2, comes immediately after their conversion. In the case of others, that joy seems delayed until after they have had an experience such as the Apostle Paul describes in Romans 7. When we cry from the heart, "O wretched man that I am! who shall deliver me from the body of this death?" then comes the answer, "I thank God through Jesus Christ our Lord." The Jews in Persia know that they had been delivered, but there is no evidence that they acknowledged the One who had delivered them.

Nevertheless they did celebrate. It was "a day of gladness and feasting, and a good day, and of sending portions one to another." This is similar to another celebration which took place in Jerusalem some years later in the days of Nehemiah. At that time "all the people wept, when they heard the words of the law." But Nehemiah said to them, "Go your way, eat the fat, and drink the sweet, and send portions unto them for whom nothing is prepared: for this day is holy unto our Lord: neither be ye sorry; for the joy of the Lord is your strength," Neh. 8:9, 10. This was not so spontaneous as the celebration in the days of Esther, but it was more spiritual. The people of Nehemiah's day knew who it was who had delivered them and had given them occasion to feast.

The Jews of Esther's day apparently took no notice of their divine Host. Many professing Christians of our day are guilty of the same omission. They celebrate Thanksgiving Day, Christmas and Easter with little or no thought of the One who gives those days their true significance. To behold non-Christians celebrating these days seems strange indeed. We who know the true significance of such days should be more careful to preserve it. In so doing we might be used of the Lord to lead others to discover the real meaning for themselves.

CHAPTER NINE 20-32 *Memorial Days*

■ THE CUSTOM of choosing certain days to commemorate special events began when the Lord set aside the seventh day to celebrate the completion of creation. When He delivered His people from Egypt and its bondage He said, "Remember this day, in which ye came out from Egypt, out of the house of bondage; for by strength of hand the Lord brought you out from this place.... This day came ye out in the month Abib," Exod. 13:3, 4. Likewise we who know Christ as Savior remember the day when we first knew the joy of sins forgiven and peace with God. For us the first day of the week on which our Lord rose from the dead will remain a glorious day.

Triumphantly we sing, "The stone which the builders refused is become the head stone of the corner. This is the Lord's doing; it is marvelous in our eyes. This is the day which the Lord hath made; we will rejoice and be glad in it," Psa. 118:22-24.

The days of which this portion speaks are not referred to in the list of holy days in Leviticus 23. None of them occurred in the month Adar, which is the last month of the sacred year. There was no conflict, therefore, with that which had been prescribed by the law of Moses. That the Jews still celebrate these days each year indicates they accept the institution as valid. Of course there is no divine directive such as in Leviticus 23, but the man who took the lead in establishing this custom was Mordecai, who at that time ranked with other great leaders of Israel.

Mordecai "wrote those things, and sent letters unto all the Jews that were in all the provinces of the king Ahasuerus, both nigh and far, to establish this among them, that they should keep the fourteenth day of the month Adar, and the fifteenth day of the same yearly, as the days wherein the Jews rested from their enemies, and the month which was turned unto them from sorrow to joy, and from mourning into a good day: that they should make them days of feasting and joy, and of sending portions one to another, and gifts to the poor," Esther 9:20-22.

Nothing is said here about the destruction of their enemies. Instead there is the meaningful expression, "The Jews rested from their enemies." How suggestive it is of that rest which the Lord Jesus gives, "Come unto me, all ye that labor and are heavy laden, and I will give you rest," Matt. 11:28. If the labor was self-imposed, one might stop at any time, but the labor was ordered by a taskmaster as real as any that the children of Israel had in Egypt. The burden was placed upon our necks by one who would have enslaved us forever. In offering us rest, the Lord Jesus offered to set us free from the domination of sin and Satan. Our Emancipator has removed our sins as far as the East is from the West,

And rest divine is ours instead,

Whilst glory crowns His brow.

When Zacharias, the father of John the Baptist, celebrated the birth of his son, he said that the Israelites should be saved from their enemies that they might serve the Lord without fear, in holiness and righteousness before Him, all the days of their life, Luke 1:71-75. Zacharias was speaking of the Messiah who alone could bring such deliverance to His people. Surely he was also thinking of more than mere human enemies. A man of his spiritual stature would never be satisfied with political freedom alone. True freedom comes from Him of whom it is written, "If the Son shall make you free, ye shall be free indeed," John 8:36.

Another characteristic of this festive occasion was the sending of portions one to another and the sending of gifts to the poor. How easy it is to observe the former as is so often done at Christmas and Easter while the latter is forgotten! Many a Christmas celebration has become nothing more than "an exchange of gifts." There is nothing wrong with such a custom, but we must not stop there. The Jews were to send gifts to those from whom they could expect nothing in return. Our Lord said, "If ye do good to them which do good to you, what thank have ye? for sinners also do even the same...

love ye your enemies, and do good, and lend, hoping for nothing again; and your reward shall be great, and ye shall be the children of the Highest: for he is kind to the unthankful and evil," Luke 6:33, 35.

How good it is to read that "the Jews undertook to do as they had begun, and as Mordecai had written unto them; because Haman the son of Hammedatha, the Agagite, the enemy of all the Jews, had devised against the Jews to destroy them, and had cast Pur, that is the lot, to consume them, and to destroy them!" As I write these words I have before me a news report published in the *Chicago Daily News* concerning the celebration of the Purim festival. Among the sermon titles, I find this one, "Are we Faced with a New Haman?" How the rabbi intended to answer that question was not indicated, but the mention of the name of Haman shows that he is still looked upon as typical of one who may be seeking the destruction of the Jewish people.

Just as the name of Judas Iscariot is associated with the worst form of treason, so the name of Haman will always stand out as the typical anti-Semite. He is here described as "the enemy of all the Jews." We must never forget that this anti-Semitism was just a part of a greater scheme to destroy, if possible, "the seed" who was to bruise the serpent's head, Gen. 3:15.

"But when Esther came before the king, he commanded by letters that his wicked device, which he had devised against the Jews, should return upon his own head, and that he and his sons should be hanged on the gallows." The name of *Esther* is not actually in the original text here. The American Standard Version rendors it, "When *the matter* came before the king." But the new Revised Standard Version has restored the name of the queen. The matter would never have come before the king if Esther had not risked her life to bring it to his attention. In the news article referred to above we find the statement that the festival of Purim "recalls the heroism of Esther, who risked her life to aid the Jewish people."

"Wherefore they called these days Purim after the name of Pur," that is, the lot. Haman and his sons meant it for evil, "but God meant it unto good, to bring to pass as it is this day, to save much people alive," Gen. 50:20. This was not the first time that the Lord brought good out of that which was designed for evil. That should comfort every child of God. Our God is able to turn the darkest day into a shining light.

"Therefore for all the words of this letter, and of that which they had seen concerning this matter, and which had come unto them, the Jews ordained, and took upon them, and upon their seed, and upon all such as joined themselves unto them, so as it should not fail, that they would keep these two days according to their writing, and according to their appointed time every year; and that these days should be remembered and kept throughout every generation, every family, every province, and every city; and that these days of Purim should not fail from among the Jews, nor the memorial of them perish from their seed."

The Jews who had passed through those dark days confirmed the reasons for the observation of Purim. They not only bound themselves to perpetual observation of these days, but included also the generations yet to come, as well as any proselytes who might join themselves to them. They included every generation, every family, every province and every city.

Christians also have a "memorial." When we break bread in remembrance of our blessed Lord, in a sense we are having fellowship with every Christian; for "we being many are one bread, and one body: for we are all partakers of that one bread," I Cor. 10:17.

Queen Esther's role in this is significant. Here she excels Ruth, the only other woman honored by having a book of the Bible named after her. Toward the close of the book of Ruth she becomes less prominent. She is passive rather than active. But in the case of Esther we find just the opposite. "Then Esther the queen, the daughter of Abihail, and Mordecai the Jew, wrote with all authority, to confirm this second letter of Purim." This is the second time that Esther is referred to as the daughter of Abihail. When she was first discovered as a possible candidate to take the place of the deposed Vashti, she was referred to as the daughter of Abihail, Esther 2:15. After that no reference is made to her father until this. Now, instead of trying to conceal her ancestry, the historian seems to emphasize it.

Even though Mordecai is referred to again as "the Jew," we never find that to be the case with Esther. When Mordecai was referred to as "the Jew," it was not always in a complimentary way. Here it is mentioned as if that were the greatest distinction he might claim. It is not by his titles that he is known here, but by his racial and ancestral connections. That which was once a reproach becomes an honor.

This is more remarkable when we consider that the letter being sent out was written "with all authority." Here one might have expected to see some title affixed. But evidently, "Mordecai the Jew" was the most dignified thing that could be said of him. Such is the case of a Christian. The most wonderful thing anyone can say about him is that he is a Christian. Even some non-Christians recognize that. All the titles and the degrees of men can never surpass the name which identifies us with Him who loved us and gave Himself for us.

"And he sent the letters unto all the Jews, to the hundred twenty and seven provinces of the kingdom of Ahasuerus, with words of peace and truth." Mordecai was more than a prime minister giving orders to those under his authority; he also was a minister ministering to the spiritual needs of his people. This is so Christlike that we cannot resist making the comparison. "The law was given by Moses, but grace and truth came by Jesus Christ," John 1:17. Thus were these days of Purim confirmed "in their times appointed, according as Mordecai the Jew and Esther the queen had enjoined them, and as they had decreed for themselves and for their seed, the matters of the fastings and their cry."

The people decreed these things for themselves and their descendants. There was perfect agreement between them and those in command. If one loves the Lord his God with all his heart and mind and soul, he will not find it irksome to keep His commandments. If that was true of those who were under the law, how much more should it be true of those whose hearts have been captivated by His love and grace? Obedience then becomes a matter of loving obligation.

That "their seed" were included shows that what was right for the parents also was proper for their children. This differs from the philosophy that we should not impose upon our children until they are old enough to decide for themselves. No one knows better what is best for his children than one who has been saved from a life of sin. He may well decree that his "seed" shall follow after him in these things. It was said of Abraham, "I know him, that he will command his children and his household after him, and they shall keep the way of the Lord, to do justice and judgment; that the Lord may bring upon Abraham that which he hath spoken of him," Gen. 18:19. That it results in blessing can be proved by scores of Christian parents who have reared their children in the nurture and admonition of the Lord.

"The matters of the fastings and their cry" remind us of the dark days when the threat of death hung over their heads. In the joy of their deliverance they could not forget what they had been delivered from. Likewise the memory of our low estate before the Lord saved us should make us grateful, as well as joyful. Wherever there has been deep conviction of sin and true repentance there will be a corresponding sense of gratitude to the Lord. It will be like the "bitter herbs" that were to be eaten with the Passover lamb. In themselves they were not pleasant to taste, but they brought out the flavor of the lamb.

"And the decree of Esther confirmed these matters of Purim; and it was written in the book." A permanent record was made of these matters so that they might be preserved for following generations. Today we still find that "the book" is referred to even by those who seem to have no appreciation of its spiritual value. But for those of us who accept the verbal inspiration of the Bible, the fact that it was written in "the book" is significant. That is the best reason that we study this book of Esther. The things which are written here were "written for our learning, that we through patience and comfort of the scriptures might have hope," Rom. 15:4.

CHAPTER TEN
The Greatness of Mordecai

■ THIS BRIEF CHAPTER of only three verses is more than an appendix to the book of Esther. Commenting on the opening verse, A. T. Olmstead remarks in his *History of the Persian Empire* that "without a word of protest, the populous and wealthy Greek cities of Asia were surrendered to a monarch whom poets and orators never wearied of describing as *the barbarian*." From that we gather that the laying of "a tribute upon the land, and upon the isles of the sea" was no more popular in those days than a similar tax would be now.

The sea referred to here is probably the Mediterranean. We can see how far west the Persian Empire may have extended. Some think that the power of Ahasuerus extended beyond the coasts of Greece to Italy and even as far west as Spain. But the eastern and western limits named in the first verse of this book of Esther give the actual extent of the empire.

One commentator takes the view that "the isles" mentioned here were islands in the Persian Gulf. But a glance at the map would hardly confirm that view. The few coastal islands there do not compare in size and importance with such islands as Cyprus and Crete in the Mediterranean. Although we cannot say with certainty which islands are referred to, the fact remains that Ahasuerus was in need of funds. According to secular history, he had projected an unsuccessful expedition into Greece and as a result his treasury was badly depleted. But for all of that his scribes were diligent in recording "all the acts of his power, and of his might...in the book of the chronicles of the kings of Media and Persia."

Even more interesting is "the declaration of the greatness of Mordecai, whereunto the king advanced him...for Mordecai the Jew was next unto king Ahasuerus." The word here rendered *declaration* is only found twice in the Old Testament, and both times in this book of Esther. The other reference is in Esther 4:7 where it is rendered *sum*. Although it refers there to "the sum of money that Haman had promised to pay to the king's treasuries for the Jews, to destroy them," it was Mordecai who used the word. But here it is used to describe the measure of Mordecai's greatness. There is something ironical about that. It sounds as though the Lord was actually making a mockery of Haman's promise. The word for *stingeth* in Proverbs 23:32 comes from the same root in the Hebrew. One can see how the declaration of the greatness of Mordecai would sting those who had sought his ruin.

But Mordecai was not only great in the court of Ahasuerus, he was also "great among the Jews and accepted of the multitude of his brethren." That must have meant a great deal to him. Often, as the Lord Jesus warns us, a man is without honor in his own country and house. But to say that Mordecai was accepted of the multitude of his brethren means that they were unanimously pleased with him.

When we think of his defiance of Haman, we can see how some of them might question his wisdom. But no one could question his courage.

The greatness of Mordecai never inflated him. He never became a megalomaniac. On the contrary, he was most altruistic, ever "seeking the wealth of his brethren, and speaking peace to all his seed." Their wealth here does not refer merely to their material wealth, but their good in its widest possible sense. By virtue of his high position and authority, he would be able to initiate legislation which would promote the well-being of the people. But he was even more than a legislator and administrator, he was a counselor and a preacher "speaking peace to all his seed."

The book closes with a living man active in the best interests of all concerned. The history of most men concludes with an obituary. Not so with Mordecai. Thus the impression is left in our minds of one who lives on and on. "He that doeth the will of God abideth forever," I John 2:17.